TulipTree review

SPRING/SUMMER 2022
issue #11

Wild Women

TULIPTREE
PUBLISHING, LLC

Contents

Ashore

Branden Boyer-White

WHAT WOULD I HAVE TOLD YOU ABOUT MYSELF, BEFORE HER? THAT I WAS thirty-three? You'd have seen for yourself that I'm a woman and heard that I'm Irish, though I'd left long ago.

That I was alone.

I suppose I'd have told you about fishing for crab.

The lobster is what Maine is famous for but I never cared to compete with the highliners. I'd always kept my operation modest and run on my own, the way my uncle had in his twelve-foot boat that he'd left me along with everything he knew. How to pace my life around the schedule of the pots, dropping them to the harbor's bottom and hauling them up full of crab to sell at the market on our small town's wharf, the rest trucked with the other local catch to a processing plant in a bigger town I'd hardly been to and sold tinned in even bigger cities I would never see. How to follow the crab to where they'd feed next, knowing our waters not only by the mountains of the coast rearing up from the sea, or the lighthouses that shone against the dark trees, but by the layers of life skittering over the sand or gliding through the sky, diving for the rest of it that lurked beneath the waves. I could set my watch by them, my fishing companions. A porpoise surfacing alongside, or a whole pod jetting by. The seals dozing on the rocks and the buoys, not stirring from their sleep when I passed as if I were nothing more than a fly idling by, used to the small motors of boats like mine. All of us used to all of it, each day like the one before, until one wasn't.

We'd had a storm overnight, so I'd set out to see how my pots had weathered it and sure enough, one had gone loose. Hoping it had washed ashore, I took my boat back and set out on foot. The beaches were a mess of birds, happily going through the delicacies the storm's surf had tossed out in its fit, including my trap, banged up but not too badly. I carried it back, clams telling of their dive away from my boots with a bubble sent up in the mud.

The tide had since gone out from under my boat, leaving her aground on the beach. I always tied her up but had never put in any sort of landing, fearing it would be an invitation for others to pull up, and though I didn't own the sheltered stretch of sand and tumbled rock standing between my house and the sea, no one came to it. I threw the pot into her and set to patching it.

I was using the spine of my knife to jimmy a buggered wire, maybe not the smartest, and when it gave, the knife flicked from my hand, arcing into the scrabble of tall rock just beyond. I swore and went after it, sucking at my thumb where it had been nicked but worrying more that the sea would dull the blade stupid against the rocks or crawl away with it altogether. That's when I saw her.

She'd crept from around a boulder tall as herself, eyes fast on me. Standing barefoot on my beach in the late morning light, she looked as old as me, or as young. She was stark naked.

I almost asked if she was alright but she startled suddenly, as if I'd done a thing to startle her, though I hadn't really, I'd just been. It made me jump in turn. We went still.

Then she tilted her head, her long hair brushing her waist like fingers. That hair was the kind of shining white of a secret, like a pearl or a cave creature, a thing so hidden from the light, it begins to make its own. But her eyes were dark. You couldn't tell pupil from iris until you were indecent close to her, which I suddenly was, pulling her jaw toward mine in a firm palm without question because the answer was already between us. Her wrists around my neck, my hands taking the slope from her back to bum and using my grip there to heft her up and in.

Kissing like the antidote to drowning.

Pulling away long enough to climb into my boat, she held out her hand to me.

She rose and fell along all of my edges, liquid and insistent as the tide. I couldn't tell us from everything else—the slide and slap of the waves, the damp of the air. The smell of the sea and sex are the same anyway, a thing you know once you've tried to catch your breath at the edge of both. We pulled the salt and water from one another.

In the after-quiet, in the slow of my heart coming to, I began to feel hers beating through my ribs as she draped over me, warm as the sun we closed our eyes against. Even as I skimmed my fingers down her back sleepily, another part of me was waking up.

What if someone had seen us? Was still seeing?

I needed my knife. I slid suddenly from under her, pulling straight what of my clothes had been tussled aside. I hopped from the boat and headed toward the place in the rocks I had seen the blade flash in its flight. She called for me to come back but I didn't answer. I hadn't thought to an after, or an again. The sight of her had soaked me drunk to the bone. I hadn't thought at all.

I SUPPOSE I MIGHT have told you about my house. Bought with my own money from years of working, the bankers had to make a call to see if they could let me sign the papers, a woman unmarried in the year of our Lord 1953. Only three rooms but impressive for the starkness of where it sits, on a great stand of rock sloping crooked-teethed onto the beach below a quarter of an hour's walk from any other home, which was why I'd chosen it. It was the most alone you could get in a close-pressed fishing town Down East, an expression I hadn't understood when I'd first come to Maine, along with so much. I'd been stunned by the way the people here lived, almost in the water itself for how near it was to the homes and shops, practically washing up through the streets, and for how dependent on it they were. In Ireland, I'd visited the sea as a child on holiday, but my uncle had taught me that in Maine, I would have to live with her.

My uncle—a quiet man who minded his own business and then some. He didn't know why I'd been sent and never asked. I sure as shit didn't tell him. I took his lessons about the crabs and helped around his home. We got on.

I'd never gotten on in town. Not with the Americans, hardened as their winters and pushing their vowels geesey through their noses, or with the other immigrants, the slants or rolls we put to our letters sentencing us to Different, no matter the Where Else we'd come from. I should have fallen in with the clutch of Irish up from the docks in Portland, but I'd been a city girl back home, all paved streets and sharp clothes, the newest luxuries. Some of the homes in my uncle's town were still lit only by oil and hearth. Some of his Irish friends called me *Siobhan* even when I introduced myself as Joan. The old ways in old tongues. At first, the churchy women stole looks at my belly, hoping for the tell—a niece suddenly appearing alone, after all. I could have laughed at the limits of their minds if I'd ever felt like laughing.

Maybe I should have listened, a little, to all of them, living with their boots in the sea, beards and lashes dusted with brine and disbelieving in city ways and technology but not in gods and ghosts. They took as fact what I'd heard as fairy tales, talking of water spirits in the same breath as the weather and warning to watch for a devil so real he'd knock on your door.

But I didn't mind them because I didn't want them to mind me. Keeping my reasons to myself was like drawing breath. Natural, necessary. My house and I were the same, that way. I didn't want to let anyone in to either.

It was only later that I would think with wonder that those were the first words she'd said to me. Come back. Wait. Crying them out from my boat as I searched for my knife among the stones and small pools the tide had left.

A shine caught my eye, just under a rock ledge near where I'd first seen her. I crouched for it but pulled back immediately when I saw an animal hunkered there, in the shadow. Or no. I looked closer. Picked it up.

It was a skin, the fur dappled gray. I turned to her, knowing what it was a heartbeat before she cried out at seeing me with it. We looked at one another, me in half my clothes and one boot, her standing in my boat wearing nothing but the sunlight and the marks of my teeth and fingers. My blood smudged her jaw where I'd touched her with my cut thumb before she'd sucked it dry.

We were two meters apart, but holding the skin I knew I still held her, my brain beating helpless with the different messages given by my eyes and touch. I smoothed my thumbs down the silken fur, then pushed up against its grain. She shuddered, feeling it.

I cast my eyes down, suddenly embarrassed by her nakedness now that there was a way to cover it. I stepped up to the boat and held the skin out to her.

"You're not going to keep it?" she asked.

I'd heard the tales, but shook my head. "It's yours."

A beat more, neither of us moving. Then she grabbed it. Amazing how she could run over the rocks on the hides of her feet that had been soft as oyster flesh in my mouth. She shook the bundle out before the first wave washed her hip-deep so for a moment I saw the skin unfurl to its full length. She dove with it, her head surfacing in the calm between breakers, hair shining with water and light, and then another wave curled over her. I watched for what I knew would happen next though if you'd asked me an hour before if it were possible, I would have laughed.

Sure enough, beyond the breakers, a seal's head appeared, turning her wide, dark eyes back to me. Then she dove for good.

I found my knife and went home.

* * *

THE FIRST GIRL I'D ever loved also had light hair but eyes to match—green, gold, and sparking. Ireland had stayed out of the war but still, when it ended we all breathed freer. I wonder if it made us brave, her and me. We were schoolmates, friends. We were seventeen. And just like in the stories, a kiss woke me. I saw that my hands had been created for her body, and my heart for hers.

Then she came to me crying on a day sudden as a slap. We were wrong, she hadn't meant any of it, we couldn't. I felt my insides go up like being bombed. I would have led an army for her if I could have figured out how. Instead, I pledged the only thing I had. Myself. We could run away together. She said it was too late. She'd told.

My father beat me to bruised. Blood from my lip, in my nose, though his hand coming down didn't hurt. She'd already broken me as much as I could break.

It was only my mother who took me to the dock where the huge steamer bellowed its wounded good-bye call. She gave me the saddest eyes, of a coward who knew she was being one. But I couldn't hate her. I was choosing, choice after choice to do, to try. To leave. You can't stay here if you're going to, my father had started, but stopped like saying it would poison the tongue from his head. So I said I wouldn't stay.

My mother handed me the bag holding the last lunch she'd ever make for me, then kissed my forehead in the same spot you get the press of charcoal from the Father on Ash Wednesday. Repent. Believe.

"I know, Joanie," she said, patting my cheek. "You can't go against your nature." Then she turned and cut through the crowd, hand pressed to her mouth, away for the home that was no longer mine.

A boat ride across an ocean the size of eternity, a ferry up a coast ragged and wild as the scar from a bite, and then a muddy footpath to my uncle's home. Three legs of a journey. I lived three years with my uncle before a wet thing hunkered in his lungs for the spring and when it left, took him with it.

The things in fairy tales happen in certain sets, cursed or charmed. A trinity, a dozen, seven. Three more years, and I bought my house and moved out of town. I didn't know I was living in such a story.

But there it was: seven hours gone since I'd watched her run into the waves. Enough sun had been lost that I'd built a fire when the door rapped. I still had the salt of her on me when I opened it and found her on my stoop. In her hands was the skin, still damp. She held it out.

IT WAS HOW SHE swam through her humanness, she told me, running a palm down my side. By feeling this form of hers with another human's as close as could be.

And true, I couldn't remember appreciating a length of leg or arm more than I did hers as they tangled with mine in my sheets. Her voice filling the quiet of my room. I understood when she told me that her craving to feel it would grow consuming when she'd been away for too long. Worth risking everything.

She couldn't say why or how. It was as it was.

It's why she'd come ashore that day, peeled herself from her other skin, and hidden it, a thing she'd done many times before. She'd been watching me in my boat on the water, and then tracked me over the beach.

"I thought you were a man. A smallish one," she said, smiling. "And then I saw."

"And you were naked as Eden."

"The way you looked at me, I could tell." She played the bones of my chest like keys. "I didn't know women like you existed."

I laughed that she had said that, to me. "Well."

"And then you kissed me," she finished. Our first story together. It made me realize what I didn't know about her, among all that I suddenly did.

"What's your name?" I asked.

"What would you like to call me?" she answered, so over each part of her I whispered every endearment I'd ever heard with no shame, a name for here, and there and under there, and she laughed and gasped and took them in like air. I thought we were playing.

But I asked her again in the morning, across the sun-lit kitchen as I wondered what she might possibly eat for breakfast. And again she said, "What would you like to call me?"

"Weren't you named when you were born?" I blushed as soon as I'd said it, having no idea if she'd been a baby, or had a seal for a dam and come out as one herself.

"I don't remember. I've never needed a name unless a human had me."

So she'd given others the answer she'd given me. "What have they called you?"

"Usually just 'selkie,' or 'girl.'"

I snorted. Of course they wouldn't think she needed a proper name for a proper human, though they'd no doubt plenty indulged in her human characteristics.

"Then Míde," she said, her tongue breaking the old name at its half, a wafer. "The last man who kept me called me that."

"My thirst," I said, tossing its meaning into the air between us, her catching it with a bob of her head. An Irishman, like me but not. I could feel his lust in the name. His need to slake, but also his longing—his love, maybe. I hated it, hated him, and for a moment, her for having borne it.

"So," I said past the hot clutch in my throat. "What do you want?"

"I suppose Míde," she finally said. "It's got water in it. Same as me."

It was like being shook awake. The sea stretched endless through the window behind her where she stood on my kitchen floor on bare feet, hair dry as kindling. For me. I went to her and bound my hands with it.

Who was I to be upset, anyway? I was bringing in my scars, too.

* * *

THE SECOND GIRL I'D loved I met at our market the year after my uncle died. She came to my stall every week, and one gray morning I said, "You must like crab, then."

"Not really," she said, and turned her eyes up at me from under her lashes like a question in a language we alone spoke. Everything fell silent around me. From that day, she was the only thing I could truly hear.

I still lived in my uncle's small house on the backstreet. She would come to me there like the stars—when it was dark and always leaving just before the light. Then she stopped coming. She wouldn't meet my eyes at the market that week, or ever again. She married a man with a large house who took her to the dances in town that they walked into hand in hand.

My heart had already had cracks in it. If I were to move fast it might break, and I had moved. I bought my house on my rock and lived there. Ten years went by like one. I had a barber who cut my hair the way I wanted without needing to say something smart, and regular customers who preferred my crab to fishermen's twice my age. My heart nice and calloused. There was nothing could get in.

When Míde came to me that evening, when she'd laid the skin in my hands so we held it between us with the doorway arcing overhead, I'd asked her, "Why?"

"You're the only one who let me go," she'd answered.

And I'd said the truth. "You're the only one who came back."

THE OTHERS HAD HIDDEN the skin from her. Part of living with them had been the constant search for it until eventually, she'd found it. Run back to the sea the way I'd seen her do. Unfurling.

She said, "I told them if they cut it up, or burned it, or sent it away, they wouldn't be able to keep me anymore."

My gut shuddered, thinking of her crisping and curling to nothing in some stove. Surely she would have died. "Is that true?"

"I can only think so. I don't know. But I mostly told them that so they'd keep it close where I could find it."

"That's smart."

"Animals are," she said. "It's humans who are dumb."

I laughed because it was true.

But we couldn't leave the skin out like a jacket just pegged on the wall. She had needs about it, about not seeing it and certainly not touching it, for the way it would pull on her if she did. It was a wonder, she said, the way she'd taken it off again so soon on the day we'd become we. A thing she'd never been able to do before—before me.

So we kept it folded and tucked at the back of a drawer with the linens. Open the drawer. Take out sheets fresh with soap and sunlight, throw them wide as sails over the mattress. Make sure we had equal edges on each of our sides. Close the drawer. Nothing more to it than that.

SHE KNEW A LOT from her other times living with a human. About cooking, but she was so shit at it, we left it to me. She had a way with her clothes already, preferring them comfortable but with a shock of useless beauty; she'd spend our crabbing money on a shawl hollering with Japanese fish meant to net the purses of summer people, and then pair it with my gardening trousers.

But I had to tell her some things she'd never had to know before. About why I lived alone and far off because of what the world was like and what it didn't like.

"I don't know why it should make a difference to them," she said. "Why?"

For that one, I had no answer.

Still, she came with me to town and followed the rules I'd given about touching and nicknames. To the gossipy folks who asked we said cousin, which was a laugh given that Míde didn't look like she shared blood with any of us workaday mortals, and certainly not with me, who could fade into a sodden old wall, no trying.

Then there were the men, the ones who growled jokes to one another at the bar, their laughter rough as their hands. The best I'd always hoped for was their dismissal, which was usually all I got, but the way they looked at Míde. You knew she was rare at a glance. It wasn't just the mishmash colors of her, or the fact of her ridiculous clothes against our town's uniform of wool caps and ashy coats. I knew what the men felt when they looked at her walking through their day because I felt it, too. The way she ran her long fingers curiously over everything. Her smile going wide, easy as a child's but with the slant of a woman's.

I couldn't breathe proper until we got back to the house. The things that made me nervous about her in the wider world I could simply love, there. Her body, soft and a little round until you held her and felt it was a layer around the purest muscle. She was made of thrash and glide. I knew she would move like a bullet fired if she were in her element.

But she wasn't. She was in my arms.

BUSINESS BOOMED. BEFORE, A strange turn in the weather could strand me with a bad catch, the crabs bidden by orders I could only guess. But Míde knew them. She showed me new places to drop my pots. I threw back some of the catch so we wouldn't draw other fishermen too close.

I'd never been much of a swimmer for myself but we went all the time. She was a thing to see. That long hair winding around her like a spell, and just under the surface, the wavery lines of her bare body, for despite my early objections, she nearly always stripped before splashing in, saying why did you buy a piece of Nowhere if you weren't going to use it? Her grace took my breath away, but she was frustrated.

"I'm so slow," she'd say even as she wove easily through the swells. She'd beg me in. I learned to not fear the water, to move with undertows instead of fighting them. To part the slimy tendrils of sea grasses with my feet carelessly, no nightmares buried within. Was that what love was? To be in the world as someone else because what they felt, you did too?

Sometimes I hoped not. I didn't want her to catch my fears like a sickness, the ones that ran to fathoms because they had to. She loved to make love in the water, and I knew that she wanted to be both of her at once. But only in the dark with no moon, I'd say yes, and only in the most secluded spots. It made night animals of us, and still, I kept my eyes open, clamped a hand over her mouth to silence her. I couldn't let her touch or press into me out there, so she'd catch her breath and lead me back to the house, lock the door behind us, and, still dripping wet but safe in the space between the walls, she'd push me onto the bed. Make a net of the sheet and throw it, wrapping me until I couldn't move or breathe from laughing, and then she'd uncover just the parts she wanted and lap at them until I had no fight left and surrendered, caught, limp. Home.

WINTERS WERE HARD ON her. The sea smoked in the cold mornings and sometimes all day like it was boiling—no place for a human to be swimming. The always-shuttered windows made the house feel smaller, and she resented staying indoors as much as that body of hers asked her to; more than once, I'd had to run outside after her with her boots when she'd been only going to the garden, which was itself covered in ice.

"You need these here, remember," I'd say, pinching her toes to warm them when she'd come inside again, and she'd make sounds like I was driving her crazy and bat my hands from her feet but smile.

On days when it wasn't storming, just cold, I'd take her on boat rides along the coast, trying to give her back some of the water.

Bundled in our second skins of hats and coats and gloves, she would tell me things about the shores we passed, about what could be found in this tidal flat or had occurred once in that cove. The lighthouses and mountains were my markers, but hers were at the water's edge or just under it. We'd lived in the same world but not at all.

"So you've seen these beaches," I said to her one ride. We'd traveled so far, I'd had to dock at a strange wharf for more gas for the motor, my cheeks skinned raw from the air. It was almost Valentine's Day.

"Of course." Her nose shone pink but she still held her face in the wind, rapture on it like a saint girl in one of my old schoolbook pictures.

"What about that one?" I pointed southeast at an island so far you couldn't see the shapes of the trees on the shore, just their color.

She gave me a look. Poor you. Trying to gain one on me.

"How far have you gone?"

"Far."

"Deep?"

"Sure. But far along, too. Humans, you don't know. You're exhausted by walking to the next town over. We could take the whole sea if we wanted. I have a different idea of far than you."

I felt a familiar creature turn slimily in my belly. The same one had stirred early on, when she'd first told me that before, it felt like if she spent ten days as a human, she would have to spend a hundred as a seal.

Before what?

She had kissed me then. Before you. Rubbed my nose with hers.

The creature in my belly was Guilt.

SHADES LURKED AT THE edges of our paradise for two. We heard it on the radio, news from far south about people having to march from city to city, fighting using their words and dignity and peacefulness against slavering dogs, water hoses turned to weapons, and crosses burned like some demon's mass. Further still, boys were dying by the groupful in Vietnam for reasons no one could even agree on while that country's own people were cut down brutishly as their forests. Listening, I'd think of other, older stories I'd long ago dismissed, of the Sluagh coming as a flock of shadows restless with cruelty to cluster around a soul and take her from her bed.

Then one night, they gathered on our doorstep. From town, so late you knew it wasn't for any daylight reason that they knocked, hollering and laughing in that scariest way men's voices tangle together.

Míde crouched to the floor, wailing. "They're after my skin!"

I didn't want to tell her she had it right, but in the wrong way. My uncle's pistol, I gave to her, and I took the shotgun, backing us into the corner of the room furthest from any window. I told her, "If they get in, wait until they're close enough that you'll be sure to hit something." It was the best we could hope for, if they got in.

After they'd tried every latch, broken a windowpane with a rock like silly children—after they'd had their fun of proving that our fear was theirs to summon any time they wanted—they left. I held her as she cried until sleep took her, worrying that this would be the thing to make her leave our dry, pinched world. But she was there in the morning filling the kettle, eyes bright and mouth full of kisses for the backs of my hands, and I remembered she'd been to depths I could only imagine. It put bold in my blood.

I waited through the next night, to be sure they weren't coming back, and on the one after I left her tucked into our bed with the shotgun and went to the bar with the pistol. More rounds. Walked into the heart of the loud, stinking hoard of them, and held up and cocked the gun with a click that cut through their side-look laughter. Said to their breath-held silence, "I live bastard alone on a fucking rock with spit to my name. I've got nothing to lose. Who of you can say the same?"

They never came again.

ALL MY CAUTIONS WERE sometimes for naught. She brought a fisherman home one summer afternoon, walking him straight into the garden where I was wrestling with our sad turnout of potatoes.

"Isn't he marvelous?" she asked me, eyes alight, and I flustered with what to say about the white-haired man smiling at her side until Míde scooped a small, shaggy dog from the ground.

The marvelous dog was Banger. The man was Gerald.

I knew Gerald faintly, a clammer I liked to buy from because his made excellent chowders. His teeth were long and wax-yellow as a horse's when he smiled, and he moved older than his years from a leg injured in the Great War. Míde was on about tea so there was no way out. I led them inside.

Gerald was a lot like me, or me before Míde—from Essex, which was to say, elsewhere, there, home, and alone on his piece of this strange shore. I think Míde had known that, because though she loved the company and playing the hostess, showing him things in the house or arranging the biscuits on a plate, it was Gerald and I who became fast. Whenever he came for tea we would talk about the things that needed talking, the marches starting up again in Northern Ireland or the latest with the Soviets or the outbreak of green crab in our waters, and Míde would smile like she'd given a present we were untying the bow from, Banger lolling shamelessly on her lap under her fingers.

I dreaded the talk of those afternoons as much as I cherished it, for the moment Gerald might ask more about where Míde came from beyond the simple, obviously false answers we'd given, or how she and I were related—or not. There was a pretending we all did, unspoken but felt keenly. If Míde touched my hand as she asked me a question, or I forgot myself and placed a palm on her back to slide past her in our cramped kitchen, Gerald glanced away, cleared his throat. In this way, it could be fine. But I waited for the change, because they always come.

THE NEW AGE WAS coming into town, slow but sure. Power lines marched along the roads orderly as soldiers. The large newspapers started to get trucked in weekly, so Sundays were like a door opening onto the whole country. I caught the fever for the modern for the only reason I would, and had a couple of men out to the house to put in a real bathtub and water heater just in time for winter. Míde would have a place to splash in when she ached for it, her own mini sea until the spring.

She hated it.

"It's not supposed to be hot, it's water," she said, looking happy as a cat would in the full, steaming tub, and whenever I suggested she try it again she would say she wasn't a carrot and didn't need to go in the soup. She took her baths cold and I sighed but there was happy in it; we had our own, other tricks, anyway.

We'd make an ocean of our sheets, tumbling and rolling through them slippery as salt-creatures, the world of proper standing and walking forgotten, our limbs winding in strange knots as though we were re-forming each other in a different gravity. Our breath held, let, as human as we could be. And it was enough.

GERALD ASKED ME OVER. He and Banger lived in a house not unlike mine, away from town, hugged in by trees at the edge of the woods just as mine sat tilting on the edge of the sea. Edge-dwellers.

He led me into the small bedroom, and I blushed seeing the sheets still twisted with the shape of his sleep. At the bedside table he pulled open the drawer and lifted out a portrait, all inky browns, and handed it to me. The photographed man wore the uniform of the Great War and the crisp-clean face of the very young.

I laughed a bit; had Gerald ever been such a looker? "This is you?"

He shook his head, eyes still on the paper face in my hands, and said, "No."

My breath left and understanding rushed in in its place. I bobbed my head. We said nothing else, and never did.

But the next time he was over, I took Míde's hand on the table between us, and stayed there. Gerald smiled so faintly you wouldn't have seen if you hadn't known to look, and asked how my pots had been.

MEN WERE GOING TO walk on the moon, so we walked to the bar to see it. The crowd was mostly us who didn't have televisions or those who did, but who wished to be in the company of others to witness such a thing. I'd worried my heart into my throat about walking in together with Míde, so obviously, but turns out it didn't matter. The air was peppered with holiday, everyone buying everyone rounds. They pressed glasses into our hands without asking, pointing to the screen above the bar and telling us not to worry, we hadn't missed it.

Then there he was, alone against the blackest black, his bulky put-on form white as the alien ground he walked on. Everyone in the bar cheered like we'd all done something, and maybe we had. Soon there were two of them on the screen, going about the tasks of their scientific work so simply, but on the face of an entire other world.

When we walked home, the sky with all its space and stars looked different—a thing we could take to and cross in ships. The moon was sliced into a crescent the way it had been every month I'd lived, but all I could see was the new knowledge I had of it. The dusty, barren surface, and the men stepping over it like magic, only not. It was. We'd seen it.

"The way they moved," I said to Míde. I tried for the astronauts' slow-floating bounce on the dirt road, grabbing her hand a moment in the safe of the dark. I felt the future in my footstep, pulling us forward light and fast. We'd gazed back at ourselves from the very moon. We'd walked into the bar and stood shoulder to shoulder like any other pair, and no one had turned. "Wasn't it something?"

She'd been quiet; I should have noticed. "It looked like they were underwater," she said.

The longing in her voice was unmistakable, and frightening.

She was drooped and fearsome restless all at once. She walked along the ruffling edge of the water like hesitating in a doorway. Whenever I asked if she wanted to swim she would say no, like a penitent drunk taking the long way home to avoid the bar. We took no rides in my boat. I thought we were making a good enough showing until an afternoon that Míde excused herself from the room and Gerald clapped a hand on my shoulder and said softly, "It will mend. Things always do." I nodded to be polite.

I returned from fishing one morning and she was gone. Not around back in the garden, not down on our beach with the birds as they picked among the rocks. The emptiness of the house kicked through my ribs straight to my heart and for the first time, I rushed to the bedroom and hauled open the linen drawer. Relief flooded my veins like a second blood when the skin was still there.

When she came home, her hair was curled crispy with having been soaked in the sea. Tangled as though she'd been in someone else's bed. The skin of her face flushed pink with how hard she had swum. Alone.

"What would you like for lunch?" I asked, and that's all. The feel of the skin still prickled on my fingers—how I'd let myself touch it a moment, possess it. Had she felt it when I had? I couldn't look at her.

"Whatever you'd like," she said, her voice a match for mine, too light. Her eyes also dancing away to anything but me.

I FELT THE SKIN humming from the dresser like a third heartbeat in our home. I made the bed myself, not wanting her to open the drawer and remember where it was, though of course she did—nonsense and wishes. We were wishing so hard that soon none of it was coming true. We fought and were sullen and still I wanted her more than breathing.

Pulling my pots, I raged in my head against all I couldn't fix, the constant scree of the sea birds like the wail of fear I could shoo away less and less. Waves slapping the prow, my boat sounded as hollow as I felt.

It was easy to go into town without her, the way we'd each retreated to the corners of our life furthest from one another. I bought a small chest of steel made for hand tools, or maybe something more precious, for it locked. Hid it beneath the clammy coils of rope in my boat. I acted the thief though I hadn't stolen from her yet.

The key I threaded on a length of cord and wore around my neck when I fished, beneath my shirt so the metal warmed with my heat. I told myself I was trying to get used to it but that was a lie—I didn't need to. With it on, I already felt calmer. It beat against the bones of my chest as I hauled the pots up, pulled out the crabs who waved their arms at me accusingly. It would be for both of us, I answered them in my head. We had a whole life we'd made.

She'd been this way for too long now. She loved tea and music and our silly tree at Christmas. She loved me. She would miss it all.

She wasn't safe out there. We knew how brutal the sea and its dwellers could be, and worse, we humans to them. I could keep her safe. I could keep her.

I'd close the key in the chest when I finished work. I wouldn't wear it home, but the ghost of it weighed on my breast at the house, going heaviest when she touched me.

SHE COULDN'T SLEEP, OR else slept nearly all day. She stared into the fire evenings, shaking her head with a small smile when I asked if she wanted a book, if I could get her something to eat. She was barely eating. Soon I wasn't much, either, my belly already full of dread.

I didn't know what I was waiting for. Why I couldn't get the skin, lock it up, put us both out of our misery. All the boundaries in my life I'd stepped over, and this one froze me.

The only thing she seemed to still want was me. Hands pulling, mouth warm, body pressing, the one way we were still the way we'd always been. But being that close to her, I was also closer to her sadness. I could feel how held-tight and worn-limp she was all at once with working to make the choice every day.

But she was still making it. Staying. And I could trust that. Couldn't I?

ONE EVENING, OUR SEVENTH year. She was gone when I got back to the house. Again, I checked the drawer, and again hated myself when the skin was there, a shadow behind the sheets.

I went out to search in the swiftly dying light. Found her a small distance away sitting at the very edge of rock before beach. Her dress pulled tight over her knees so she could bundle her feet in the hem, hair wild down her shoulders like a ragged shawl. Nearly not blinking with watching the water.

"I can't come back in the house," she started before I could. "I can't stand to be in there with it."

She shook her head, her teeth chattering—shaking with holding her want back, I knew. I'd shaken like that in my life. I cast around but the land, the sky, was silent. There were no answers in the world, not in this one, ours, anyway. The moon raised its brow over the far edge of the sea like it had been hiding in her depths all day.

"I need you to hide it," she said then. "Someplace I won't think to look. Put it in that box you got, bury it."

I felt slapped with my own shame that she knew, but also not surprised. We each knew every corner of the other. "I'm sorry, Míde."

"Please," she said. Turned her impossible-dark eyes up. "Do it for me. It's my choice. I want to stay here."

It was everything I wanted. She married me, in that moment. I slipped my hand into hers and pulled her up, leading her back to our house.

WE DOZED ONLY IN snatches that night. I watched her when she slept, breathing her in, and when I drifted off I could feel she'd awoken to study me. Otherwise, over the hours, I loved every inch of her. Each long finger and toe, the soft skin behind her knees, her pulse in the deep clefts of her throat.

When the windows began to light, she pulled me from the bed. "I'm going outside," she whispered. "Let's do it now, together." Then she slipped away, leaving me to my task.

The drawer creaked loudly in the silence of the house.

She sat on the edge of my boat, the hem of her dress dark with the lick of the tide, watching the water but no longer shaking. Holding the chest. When she turned at my footfall, she wouldn't look at the skin, lifting her chin and locking her eyes onto mine.

I took the chest from her and tossed it into the boat. She startled at the crash of it and turned back to me. I shook my head. "You know you can't stay."

She cried then, and set me going. "Joan."

"And you know I won't make you. And that's the only way." Our devil's deal that we'd made that night she knocked on my door, come for its pay. The trade that had made us possible also making us impossible.

I held the skin out to her. When she took it, I saw her go limp with relief even as another current of her lit up. She nuzzled it, then shook it loose. I'd forgotten how long it was—longer than she was tall, in this form that I knew as well as my own and wouldn't again.

Suddenly, she ducked into my boat. She knew it well, the order of my life, so it was quick, her finding my knife. Before I realized what she was set on, she'd pierced a hole into the skin and began to slice through.

I cried out in time with her. The way her body tightened, hip jerking, I knew she felt it there and hollered again, grabbing for the knife.

She'd taken a small square from the skin that she folded into my hand. Her face gone ashy, her breathing heavy.

"Now you can't—" I started. But there was the truth: that the time in my life when she was mine to worry about was at its end.

We grabbed and held one another hard, even as it hurt more to take one last of what we were losing. She pressed her lips to my fingers. "I'll always," she said.

"I know," I said. "Me too."

When she kissed me I didn't feel it, my mind so frantic to catch all of it for holding that I caught none. She backed away down the beach, then turned to the water and began peeling the dress from herself, and her nakedness was the only thing that mattered. I looked at as much of her as I could. She began to run, limping with her hurt but still running as she got closer to the water—it pulled her, you could see it. Anyone could have.

When she splashed in, the skin in her hands, the waves coming to collect her, I was there again on the beach that first day I'd ever watched her. Her disappearance beneath the breakers. Then the smooth, silver head surfacing, the dark eyes locking on mine for a heartbeat, two. Then the beach empty but for me. My boat tilted among the rocks, ready for tomorrow's tide. I sat on its prow watching the water, not counting the hours, and sometime, went home.

IT'S BEEN A DOZEN years, but so far, there's no magic in the number. I don't expect any—just that what was always going to be, will. There's new gray at my temples and I had to buy glasses from the drugstore for reading. Any winter now, my hands will flare with ache in the cold. I can already feel them thinking about it at moments as I fish.

Town is changing, too, growing and hollowing out all at once. The long-timers complain that no one is staying and they mean their children; they complain that too many are coming and they mean everyone else. I see it when I visit Gerald at the group home while the nurse goes about her works quiet as a spirit, giving us our privacy that isn't. The room too hushed with the absence of Banger's feet, rest his marvelous soul. Beneath the window, so many cars go by. The last of the mud roads was paved over years ago. A big chain grocery store opened by the highway, but down at the wharf, our market goes on, for we still pull the freshest creatures from the water. I sell to more restaurants now, too, for those are popping up fast and the fancy chefs want the fanciest seafood for the summer people who pour in every season. Some stay. They build huge homes on the shore that I can see from my boat, paint shining brighter than the lighthouses that have been darkened or torn down.

My house is still far away on its rock. The space has bought me time and I'm still alone. Mostly.

There are women, once-in-a-while ones whose eyes catch on mine in town, who suddenly appear at my side and let me know in some way. They're usually young; that's when we're bravest, after all.

It's as brief as it is lovely, always, because I keep it that way. Some ask to stay, seeing in my small house on my lonely rock a great romance and not realizing they're only hearing the echo of the one that already was. Some cry and even slap me when I answer, saying they'll die if I won't have them and I tell them it just seems that way now, you'll be amazed at what you can live past.

But usually, they're as happy to leave as they were to arrive. I'm just one adventure of their many, their new boldness about it hanging on their clothes and very manners, especially if they've come from cities, but mostly because time is passing and bringing change with it. I won't see the world as different as I know it's going to be, the future rushing toward us, or us rushing into it. I suppose I wish I would get to.

Or maybe I've already seen more than most will.

The cut piece of the skin has shrunk to a littler smaller than the pocket on a man's shirt. The fur still glossy silver. I have a length of cloth that I wind snug around my chest, and beneath the first wrap, I press the piece of her next to my own skin. Tuck the cloth's end in, finish dressing, and set out for the day's work.

The other lives that were always here, more in and of the water than even us Mainers, crawl and soar and swim on. You can set your watch by them. The seals still laze in their piles on the shore, spine to spine, or wound around one another. You can tell the older ones by their size, a quality you almost can't describe—as though they've overtaken even themselves and are longer than you'd have thought possible. Their coats are changing colors, too, lightening to russet, a final flare before the fade.

There is one like this, with the thinner, elegant head of a female. I've come to know the look of her among all the others even without it, but I always check for the scar at her side. The bare, knotty flesh glistens pearly in the afternoon light, healed well but never faded.

I stop a while, whenever I see her, to watch her sleep. Her peace. The sun and wind wash over her, and the salt of the water rises into my breath like I know it's in hers where she lies dreaming, or not. I couldn't know. She doesn't open her eyes and turn them to me, and this is fine. I hope she won't, in fact—I think it would undo me.

And anyway, it is enough, this. Sun, salt, wind, water. It is enough to let her be.

Divorce Slut

Ashley Michelle C.

we fucked
like country teenagers
in the hay
fingers touch
— 2, 3, 4
permission granted
hometown smut,
homegrown slut
a gentle touch rhythmic [i n h a l e] breath
an [e x h a l e] anchor
amidst the white capped
waves where
I caught 72 white fish
off the surface
in the blink of an eye
we fucked
as adults who remember
how to play
that two
fingers in places forbidden
can be glory
by god and jesus himself
if the ladies back home

knew just how it was
you made me come
they'd pray for me
and touch themselves
in the darkness of night
beside their husbands
who had heard of the
so-called clitoris
but lost
and gave up
you have to ask for what you want
said the wise man
standing
1 foot = 30 cm
away from my aging bosom
an uncomplicated bit of advice
to ease shuffle slide
back into pleasure
crazy arms
like sawdust on a dance floor
you said face down
ass up in the air
would you mind
pulling my hair
choking me a bit
just for fun
just for lust's sake
and because death
is so similar i hope
when i die and go to heaven or to texas
the devil himself will make a trip just to say
you were a good woman but a very bad girl,

heaven, get this bitch a hamburger

and an ice cream swirl

a matter of fact

held me close

a so-called complicated man

i said i wanted pleasure

eyes raised to see yours

how they didn't blink when you said

if it's sex you want, i can give you that.

ourbodiespressed

s l o w l y

breathing

s l o w l y

the rise and

f a l l

anticipation

fear

How do you even begin to kiss?

open

to interpretation an open

relation

ship to carry me to the places i longed for when i

stared out that window

the cypress blowing in the winds of jalisco

the cornfields barren

dust in eyes close them

where seeds are planted

pumped with fuel to manipulate

nature to be just so

what is it about that assurance

the dominance

that humans so desire

i want to submit to this dark, handsome stranger
fear of falling
things fall down
fall apart
i fall to p i e c e s
each time i think about how
i haven't fallen to p i e c e s
since i opened the door and
left because it's
right to follow your gut
there is a man who has cried for me that loved me
there is a man who has put his head on his mother's lap and wept
when the curtains were drawn
i wasn't that woman
your imaginary life
built on pills
and poetry
and images on film
or horses
and ranches
where men do the talking
or warehouses
of academic lit
and that cold metal desk
or mathematical
equations
to find
the tensile strength
you lacked
what remained of the past
has been packed away
smoke filled bars

drunken laughter

tears and promises

memories I can't forget

but one day I may

fall to pieces

into the songs we sang

i fall

to bits

and pieces you mold

with your hands

wise and practiced

maneuvers dreamt by the devil himself

thank god i gave up religion when i was seven

and I'm alone

happy as I was

a girl sitting in the arched boughs

i imagined my freedom

in a cherry stamped gown

one day in the future when I could stop being a child

look at me now, mom!

i'm a real woman!

divorce slut and

self-aware

i use my words

to make poems

about how I use my words

for good love [if you want someone to _____ your _____,

    use your

words!]

moving our hands

in the rhythms of pleasure

bent over,

turned sideways
straddling
against each other
knees to ears
wrists in hand
devouring
flesh like it was the last fish fry on earth
that was nice, the time
you gave me head
and listened
carving space
to
fill
carnal voids
lip, smack, chicharron, crack, finger, fuck, want a nut?
and so it is
and so it shall be
for an uncomplicated
unwed woman like me.
Amen.

Magic

Janet Ruth

The holy woman and the bruja loved me very much,
and in the blended mystery they wove, I learned to pray.
The four corners of my world, framed by their magic touches.

The sacred and the heathen merged within their clutches.
They molded me like potters shaping a bowl of clay.
The holy woman and the bruja loved me very much.

Hallowed hands and sorcerer's charm conspired—never too much—
when I fell short of the dreams they dreamt for me, or strayed.
The four corners of my world, framed by their magic touches.

Incense smells and secret spells spilled from the magic hutch
of light and darkness in the hall, mixed into shades of gray.
The holy woman and the bruja loved me very much.

I smile at faintest memories that glimmer. It was such
a long time ago that this wise couple set me on the way.
The four corners of my world, framed by their magic touches.

I learncd to love the sacred and the wild beneath their watch,
and still, I love them both—a world within myself—today.
The holy woman and the bruja loved me very much.
The wholeness that is my world reflects their magic touches.

Monarch

Emily Jon Tobias

TWO HUNDRED EIGHTY-FOUR POUNDS, AND COUNTING. THE SCALE CREAKS under the weight of Georgia's bulging thighs, trunk-like arms, abundant folds of flesh where lint and hair live. Her chins make for a blurry line of sight when she looks down, her toes barely visible beyond. She steps off the scale and wraps herself in the oversized bathrobe. Gripping the sides of the sink to brace herself, she looks dead into the mirror. "Good," she says into ocean eyes. "It will finally fit."

That Frank is waiting in the next room, behind a closed door, gathers as a kind of pressure just below her left eye. A twitch, but nothing more. Georgia's accustomed to the weight of distance between them, the empty space.

"Are you going to get dressed anytime in the next hour? The guys are meeting us for drinks at six."

"If you're in a rush, I can just meet you there," Georgia says.

In the next room, out of eyeshot of the woman, the man picks at his clothes, impatient, calls out, "Weren't you the one that wanted me to take you with this time? Jesus, Georgia, just put your fucking clothes on and let's go." She senses her husband's brusque hustle, pictures him huffing from off the bed as he shoves feet into his boots, stomps across the room toward the front door. She knows he always grabs a beer, pops the top off from an old opener attached to the wall under a hook holding his keys. This time's no different. With one swoop, he's got both in hand.

Oh, she can hear his temper rising, even from this distance, through closed doors, still she lets the robe unravel itself, opening down the front. Freed, her breasts roll down her ribcage, landing just above the belly button. She turns to the full-length mirror propped behind the scale, stance pried open. Her reflection spills over the mirror's edges so that she can't see her arms as the robe slides from her shoulders. She reaches down, pulling up on her belly so she can get a closer look at the curly hairs that weave around her crotch. Leaning in, she struggles to remember just how long it's been since she's been touched down there. *Too long to remember*, she thinks, and reaches in the cabinet for her Hershey's stash, hidden among the tampons.

"Georgia, let's go," Frank yells from outside the door.

A twinge of cigarette smoke floats into the open bathroom window from outside where Frank is still waiting. She crinkles her nose; the corners of her mouth turn down. His smoke disgusts Georgia more than the smell of overcooked vegetables enforced by her mother in her youth. When the girl was nine, her mother decided they would diet together after finding Halloween candy stashed under the girl's bed that she'd retrieved from the trash bin outside.

"Georgia," her mother said, "sit up. No slouching. I need to explain something to you."

The girl sat straight-backed on a tall stool in the middle of the kitchen while her mother talked, one hand to hip, a finger wagging in the girl's face. She explained what trouble Georgia had been for her during childbirth, how her birth was an excruciating labor of pain and tears that lasted forty-six hours because of the girl's nine pounds, eight ounces of baby body. That she'd suffered for weeks after, even months, while Georgia's father took over all household responsibilities. She went on about the depression, the devastating sadness of trying to connect with her tormented child. How bonding with the baby took real, concerted effort, like cramming for an exam. When the child wouldn't take her breast, the mother was expected to know all the answers. A forced bonding, her mother said, that turned her nipples raw and swollen, an attachment that almost killed her.

"Georgia, your eating has gotten completely out of control," her mother warned.

"I'm sorry, Mommy."

"I will not allow for a complete letting go."

"I will get skinny. I promise, Mommy."

"I've worked too hard, suffered too much."

"I will get ahold, Mommy."

"That's right, child, we have *got* to get a grip."

Georgia left the kitchen that day grateful she hadn't killed her mother, more willing than ever to restrict herself. Soon after, the mother held her daughter's slack hand leading her into their fifth Weight Watchers meeting together. Georgia had learned how to fool the weight coaches. When the woman's back was turned, she would shimmy her body to the outer edge of the scale and lift one leg just slightly, toes balancing above, unnoticeable to her coach. This time, her scheme lost her a good five pounds when the scale settled. The coach was thrilled. Her mother high-fived the woman, gleaming, while Georgia stood aside, fidgeting with the zipper on her jacket.

"We are all so proud of you, Georgia," the coach said. Her mother approached then with light in her eyes, a brightness Georgia had never seen before. The woman smiled wide. There was warmth around her when she got down on one knee to help zip the girl in. The mother tucked a strand of hair behind the girl's ear, patted her on the head. Then, she ran her hands down the front of the jacket, drawing it together around Georgia's mid. Too tight. Her mother tugged. Georgia blushed, sweat gathering on her nape. Her mother pulled harder. She stretched the fabric from back to front, trying to make it fit. When the woman realized she'd been duped, her mouth crumpled into a cutting frown. She snatched the girl by the wrist and dragged her to the car, forcing a smile at the room on the way out.

At home that night, Georgia cried when her mother forced her onto the scale. Proof of the girl's indulgence was in. She begged for the forgiveness of her sin. When her knuckles were rapped by the fork's steel tines, she watched the skin on her hands swell then shrink, puckering around each little wound. "Maybe this will teach you the importance of limits," her mother said. Later, she'd be reminded of those red welts by the stretch marks along her belly, her thighs, her biceps, all her undersides. Tagged by the limitation she had always lacked.

In the bathroom, she still smells Frank smoking. Georgia's knuckles go white as she clenches her fists. Her body's an arsenal of anger, enough stored for a fallout shelter with full reserves, but the weight, the weight she carries in pain and pounds somehow softens her sorrow, consumes any energy leftover for a fight. She releases her fists, watches her palms go red again. Surplus feelings are stuffed like dressing, then left to bloat.

"Coming, I'm coming." Georgia pinches the white tag of a Kiss, peeling it slowly. The aluminum spreads back from around the melting piece. Her lips turn up into a soft grin. She sticks out her tongue to catch the Kiss off her fingers. The chocolate is so close to her mouth now, she can already taste it when, suddenly, it slips from her hand, plunging into the toilet below. Georgia heaves herself forward, shoves her arm into the water. "No, no, no," she says, fishing the bowl. She swims her hand around in a futile attempt to recoup her loss until the water streaks brown.

As the candy dissolves, Georgia's heart pounds. She braces herself, both hands on the edges of the toilet seat. When she slides to her knees, her head comes forward, and a tear comes off her chin, released to join the waters beneath. She hears Frank's voice then, from way back, echoing against the rim of the toilet bowl. His voice, low and constrained, at midnight, after all the commotion was over, "What the fuck happened, Georgia?" Drenched, she stood before him while he sat on the edge of the bed, jacket still zipped, elbows to knees, staring at his shoes. Wadded at his feet, the pamphlet from the doctor on postpartum depression.

October 10. Pacing the room, she told her husband what he needed to know, recounting the relevant details as if a confused witness to an unsolved case. Georgia had clothed her child in a tiny pink swimsuit and T-shirt given to her by Frank's mother that said MAMA'S GIRL in bold block letters. To keep the child's hair from her face in the heat, she grabbed a bright pink silk scarf handed down from her mother the night of prom with Ernesto Garcia when she squeezed into the golden dress for a snapshot, praying to be queen for just one night. "For God sakes, Georgia, suck it in, can't have you spilling all over the place for the shot. Turn to the right, so I can get your good angle. Don't breathe. Suck it in. Now smile, Georgia. One, two, three, say cheese." Her mother tied the bright pink silk scarf around Georgia's waistline like a sack of potatoes, the same bright pink silk scarf Ernesto Garcia plucked at nervously to get up her golden dress later that night.

With the child at her hip, off they went, the bright pink bow bouncing with each step down the weathered wooden stairs, blue door left ajar. Rows of agave and octagon succulents lined the sloped sidewalk to Baby Beach. Late fall red spikes sprouted from the middle, as the dead outer leaves gave way. Georgia looked past the neon birds of paradise, with their proud plumes and orange manes. She didn't catch the hummingbirds sucking on fuchsia trumpets or tiny baby lizards eyeing her from the cracks in concrete. When the monarchs swirled around her daughter's crown, she shooed them away, flipped her child from one side to the other. The child's bare feet dangled, one at Georgia's front, one at her back, as her tiny hand tightened around Georgia's clammy shirt right at her mother's heart.

On the sands of Baby Beach, she sat cross-legged facing the water with her daughter in the cave between her knees. She wrapped her arms around the girl, felt jailed by the child, caged by her own misshapen after-birth body. Baby Beach with its confection of perfect sugary bodies—coveted, lovely bodies. Unrestricted bodies.

She scooped up her daughter, cradling her like an infant. Ocean foam crept over Georgia's toenails, as she stood with the child in the cocoon of her arms, rocking back and forth, stepping into the swells. "Hush, baby, hush," she whispered. "Everything is going to be okay, baby." One foot in front of the other until the incoming tide reached her knees, and as the salt bath touched the bottom of the child's tiny pink swimsuit, the girl turned curiously silent, buoyant, lighter. Georgia unraveled her arms, placed one palm at the small of the child's back, the other at the nape of her neck. The water reached Georgia's waist, and the ocean floor turned from sand to rock.

Baby girl floated. Like an island over the hump of each wave until Georgia barely held her at all. Georgia's feet floated free of rock and sand, and the girl cooed, clouds reflecting in an ocean just like her mother's eyes. Georgia pinched the tip of the bright pink silk scarf that crested in a bow at the top of the girl's head, pulled it back—like peeling a Kiss—the bow unraveled into Georgia's hand, baring the child's forehead for Georgia to lean in with a kiss. Weightless.

Georgia told Frank how the onlookers were full of pity more than shock. She could tell by the way they embraced one another, as if huddling around a campfire, eyes soft and drooping. She didn't question the authorities when they questioned her so little. It was clear they saw the disheveled, drenched look of her, believed she couldn't possibly be in her right mind. The rescue team spent more time asking her if she was certain she *had* a child than actually looking for the girl. When the EMT found her heart rate remarkably steady, Georgia pinched herself to get the blood flowing. She wanted to give the people the sorrow and fear they expected. Those crowds with their perfect sugary bodies came to soothe rather than scold, touching her back, shuffling around, offering drinks of water, a towel, a seat. Georgia tried to cry, to wither, to talk herself into the accident. And the truth of it was that Georgia didn't *quite* mean to let go all the way. But she certainly didn't mean to hold on either. She never intended to have to choose. Somehow, bearing down on her daughter in those moments of weightlessness seemed too fierce, too primal, to be right. In the end, the way she saw it, holding on was simply . . . unnecessary. It seemed to her that the sea could take care of both of them, had a better handle on it than she ever could.

When she was finished, Georgia stood still. She stopped talking. Looking to Frank, she held her breath, waiting for his reaction. He lifted his head, straightened his spine. "We will never speak of this again," he said. Then, he stood up and walked out of the room past her, brushing his hand along her shoulder. That was the last intentional touch of kindness Georgia can remember.

Georgia stands. She flushes the toilet. Then, she unwraps another Kiss. Naked and loose, she devours the chocolate in one slurp, and with the sweetness lingering on her tongue, she hobbles toward the bathroom door, the last bits of sugar dissolving along with her moment of escape. She considers picking up the pace as she eyes the small safe collecting dust in the corner of their one-room, second-floor, seaside apartment. After careful consideration, she decides to take her time.

In the closet, she can see the progression clearly. She runs her hand over the hangers of size eight flowery sundresses, passing by each outfit, up in size for each year of the Gaining. Her fingers snag on skinny straps, pluck through wide-banded elastic polyesters, all in a nice row. Passing through time this way, Georgia catches the scent of her daughter caught in the folds of slimmer summer linens. Mornings, when the baby would tuck into her chest, Georgia breathed in the scent of new skin behind her tiny ear. She smelled like freshly baked cookie dough and plastic, sweet and clean. Once upon a time, before the Loss, all three of them lay together until noon on some Saturdays. Their rumbling bellies didn't matter and Georgia craved nothing more than what she had at that very moment. Phone calls from family and friends were left unanswered. Back then, Frank could wrap his body around her, even as she wrapped hers around the baby, like he was the pod protecting its peas.

They used to respect one another, before the Loss, before the agreed silence and mutual loathing. For their first date, all those years back, he'd taken her for a picnic along the Pacific shore. He spread a blanket out for her against the waterline, set out tropical fruits and fancy crackers with spreadable cheese on little paper cocktail plates. Then, he prepared the snacks, feeding them to her from his fingertips right to her mouth. When he said, "You are gorgeous, Georgia," his voice was soft and easy as the roll of the sea.

"Georgia, seriously, move your big ass. One more smoke, and I'm leaving, with or without you." Frank peers in through the window to check on her and lights another one. She knows he can't stand how slow she's become. Control of him with such little exertion is something she's come to enjoy. Her sloth eats at him, and Georgia certainly doesn't mind.

She finds the outfit at the very end of the rod, still wrapped in a plastic garment bag from Dressbarn. She snips the red sale tag with a nail clipper, and as $39.99 flutters to the carpet, she unzips the dress, holding it wide in front of her so she can step in. With both feet planted through the bottom, she gathers it up, and stretching hard, slinks the dress around her middle like stuffing sausage into its casing, until finally, after some hard work, the straps balance on her shoulders landing the swooping neckline in place, just above the cavern of her cleavage. Fuchsia flowers turn light pink, stretched as they are against her widest parts, while the white beneath them holds thin and sheer. The bottom hem falls just above her doughy knees, and as she pulls on the edge to make more space, she realizes that she won't be able to reach the zipper.

"Frank," she calls out the open window, "I need your help in here."

By the time Frank is behind Georgia, she has put on the final touches, a bright pink silk scarf tied into a big bow at the crown of blond, messy curls. She looks like Shirley Temple in a funhouse mirror, everything so enlarged that Frank's head seems to be coming out of her shoulder at the neck, no body to be found. He treats Georgia like an overstuffed duffel bag, pressing her back fat in where the zipper is too tight. Skin catches in the zipper's teeth as he forces it upward—stuffs, zips, stuffs, zips, until finally, there's a slack in tension and her upper back gives enough space for landing. He says he could have used a second man for the job.

"Sick," Frank says, sweat beading at his brow, "Just gross."

Georgia takes one last look in the mirror and cocks her head like a Spaniel. Finds that she agrees in part with him, discovers she's also quite content with how much progress she's made. Georgia's body is, to her mind . . . fulsome. It reminds her of the way her name looks on paper, round with full G's and voluptuous vowels. Way before the Loss, when she was smaller, Georgia had often wished she had a name like Lilly. An upright, slender name, all I's and L's. A name like Lilly would suggest that she smelled nice and had a pretty feel to her while Georgia, on the other hand, made people think of a place full of sweat and fried food. Maybe that's been her problem from the beginning, why she always felt out of place. She never fit into her name. Until after the Loss, that is. Well into the Gaining came the understanding that her grief needed an entire sea, not some little puddle. No, Georgia's heart needed space to shatter. Especially if she cracks the safe gathering dust in the corner that stores the single leftover from the Loss, airtight and fireproof. The other effects of mourning are ingested—each Coca-Cola a river runoff; every Kiss, a sprinkle of sand; each Twinkie, a life raft keeping her afloat. The way Georgia sees it, this is how she was always meant to be, given the way things turned out.

On the porch railing, a monarch hovers and lands. Instinct guides the small kaleidoscope to winter over in California warmth, but this one has traveled off course to deliver a message. Georgia misses the point as, eyes on Frank, she follows her husband down the weathered wooden stairs.

Georgia bobs along behind Frank down the street toward the corner bar. They walk, a smart choice given Frank's inclination to overdo it. The short jaunt leaves Georgia breathless and achy, so she lets distance gather between them. The farther away he gets, the easier Georgia breathes. A million tiny beads of sweat lubricate her limbs, but nearby, the ocean blows rich, soothing aromas, a breeze that wafts against her bare skin, ballooning the dress a smidge in the middle—a pleasantry afforded her by the special dress she chose for the big outing. Georgia's mouth waters with the sting of salty air against chafed thighs. She enjoys the irritation. Since the Loss, Georgia covers herself, seeing no need to disturb others. The Gaining is to show the world how sorry she is, but the freedom the dress provides in this moment is so delicious, she can't help but feel content. Her heart slows, and between the thumps, she hears the silence after the crest of each tumbling wave.

"Hey you, want a ride?"

Windblown surfers idle beside her in a topless Jeep. Georgia drops her handbag, startled. The youngsters, two young boys with two girls to match them, strike Georgia as simply glorious, half-clothed, bronzed and baked to perfection. She bends to retrieve her fallen bag, and as she stands, the skirt shimmies to just beneath her bottom.

The girls snicker, covering their mouths, while the driver continues, "You look hot. You need a ride?"

Georgia tugs down on her dress, considering her options. During the Gaining, Georgia has limited options, and, in the process, decision-making has been made easier. She doesn't have to decide what to wear when nothing fits; she doesn't choose food when more is all that matters; doesn't worry about making Frank happy when nothing will. The Gaining keeps Georgia safe, enclosed.

"Thank you for asking, but I'm due to meet my husband and his pals just down the street for drinks. He was walking with me, but I got behind."

One of the girls throws her head back in dramatics. "Well, I wonder how that happened."

"I'm pretty slow."

"I can see that."

All eyes are on Georgia. She reddens from the heat of standing still. Georgia understands this crew is sickened by her. She knows that their offer is a ruse.

The surfers jiggle in the rumbling Jeep, waiting for Georgia's response. Prince Charming reaches into a greasy McDonald's paper bag on the dash and stuffs a french fry into his mouth.

"Want one?" He grabs the bag and shoves it across his princess's lap toward Georgia. "Or a handful?"

"How about the entire bag? I don't see the need for just one when it comes to fries," Georgia says.

"Well that's obvious."

"Is it?"

"You're huge, don't you see that?"

"I do."

"Don't you care what you look like?" Charming's white wife beater hugs his rippled abs, each muscle a dune Georgia imagines his girlfriend ploughing over. Georgia would rather knead his belly like dough, watch it stretch and spread.

"The bigger, the better," she says, reaching for the bag, but the driver snatches it back. He balls it up, wringing out the brown paper soaked in grease, and shoots it in Georgia's face. Ketchup splatters across blonde curls as the bag bounces off her forehead, landing at her feet. A humid eighty-seven December degrees has melted Georgia's makeup into pan-fried butter. Georgia looks down at the pile of fries at her feet.

"Such a waste," she says, tonguing the salt on her lips.

"We're out of here. Let's cruise." Tires screech as the princess waves like a queen while their ride folds into the road ahead.

"What a mess," Georgia mumbles, brushing crumbs down her front.

She sighs. All the theatrics are a waste on her. Hostility is merely a formality. She knew what the Gaining would mean, even before the Loss, has known ever since childhood. Georgia's mother took her to Sears to buy her first training bra the summer before fifth grade. On the first day of school, Mrs. Ness assigned Georgia a front row seat, the straps of her training bra visible to the entire class through her white T-shirt she wore. "Georgia Porgia has boobs. Pass it on," whispered one kid to the next until Georgia felt holes burned in her back by their stares. When Georgia came home after school that day in tears, her mother suggested a baked potato diet, all the rage in the early '80s. "Maybe if you can just get a handle on this baby fat issue, Georgia, the kids will be friendlier." Georgia desperately wanted a handle, and to please her mother, so she decided to give it a try.

That was when she learned how to count calories. Two hundred seventy-nine calories per large potato, leaving enough calories for the six home-baked chocolate chip cookies she ate while hiding in the TV room. The next day she ate only half a baked potato—no butter—to make up for her cookie wrongdoing. The handling worked. If she gave up a meal, she got a kiss on the lips from Danny Boomer. Sacrificing food for a whole day meant he tongued her in public rather than stuffed in the gymnasium broom closet. For the high school prom, if she snorted enough to stay high and hungry for two days, she won the crown, not for prom queen but from the Burger King where Ernesto Garcia fondled her in the boys' bathroom stall as though he loved her.

Georgia bumbles toward a storefront business, leans in to use the shop window as a mirror, knowing that at the very least, her lipstick needs touching up. In the warped reflection, even fingers and elbows, her sharpest angles, seem more obtuse. She ruffles around crusty ketchup to puff up her crown, rounding out the bow. With L'Oréal in hand, she leans in face-first, close enough to fog the window with her steamy breath. She shields her eyes to get a better look inside.

Just beyond the glass there is row on row of home furnishings, wicker sofas and plastic chairs, tables with lamps glued to the tops, all made cheap by Asian children in a land far, far away from the rich seaside town. Georgia puckers her red lips against the glass leaving a mark she assumes no one will see. As she pulls back, a man appears out of the void in the near distance. Dust balls hang from his broom, and when he looks up, Georgia sees his face flash white in the dark. He stalls a moment, then his hand rises as if pulled by a string, in something like a wave.

He mouths a message to her, "Hello, how do you do?" sculpting each syllable with his mouth to make sure she understands. Yes, she thinks, a tidy man. Neat in his clothes and steps, something exact about his manner—fastidious, careful. Her culinary judgments are immediate. With a starched shirt like that, this one must eat meals on a tight schedule. Oatmeal for breakfast at 8:30, carrots and bologna sandwich on white for lunch at 12:30, and spaghetti for dinner most nights, anywhere between 6:00 and 6:15 in the evening. Her hunch is that he's worn the same leather belt for decades, never gains, never loses. She doesn't realize how close she has come to the truth of this sparse man—his attention to detail, the rigor with which he lives his life. All she genuinely knows for the moment is that he is a pantomime window washer, which she finds particularly silly, and in truth, quite endearing. He sticks up his pointer finger, crooks it toward the shop's front. She nods once, and he bolts toward the front where he waits with the door held open.

"Well, hello there," he says. "And your name is?" His voice is deep, so full it doesn't suit him, much too loose and roomy for the scrawny man Georgia sees. She delights in his sound like creamy chocolate mousse—rich, airy.

The way he eyes her reminds Georgia of how kids watch cartoons—enchanted, eager, like she's the centerpiece of his smorgasbord. She wonders if this petite man wants to devour her. Would he let her dribble down his chin? He would have to wear a bib, which she presumes wouldn't suit him, although she's certain the mess would suit him less. She's right, about how looking at her makes this man want to break all his own rules.

"Georgia," she says.

"How do you do, Georgia?"

"How?"

"Yes, how." He takes a step closer.

"Perhaps you saw the french fry massacre from the other side of your window."

Only then, it seems, he notices the dried ketchup at her hairline, just above the right temple. "I feel like I just stepped into a dream," he says.

"Well, I suspect I just might have, too. Anything's possible."

"I thought I recognized you from somewhere," the man says.

At the halfway point between them where their eyes meet, somewhere close to the bright pink bow atop Georgia's head, the air thickens. Something invisible is suspended between them—dense enough to ripple, light enough to float.

"Walk with me, Georgia." The man reaches around the door, flips the open sign to show closed, and locks up. "I'll take you wherever you need to be." He offers an arm.

Georgia looks toward the bar. She thinks of Frank, the darkness inside, the low lights and grungy floor. Then, she looks up to the heavens. One cloud softens above her. The sky sweeps the wisp into the shape of an angel right before her eyes. Suddenly, she can't imagine being enclosed just yet. No, she craves winter winds off the tide. Today, she longs to be outside.

Georgia hooks her arm in the bend of his elbow as he ushers her down the street toward the bar. She feels lighter next to him, as if they're floating, with her body tucked under his wing. The palm trees they pass are dressed up as candy canes in Christmas lights, looking strangely misplaced in afternoon sun and winter heat. They take the long way, strolling through the Lantern District, along Del Prado, window shopping. Georgia keeps her eyes down, relishing each step with this man beside her. They smile gently at each other when they pass the American flag staked outside the old hardware store as if remembering a shared, unspoken past.

Walking next to him, this stranger, this man with his small walk and clean smell, Georgia floats away from the sea of space.

On approaching Rita's Diner, he stops, turns to Georgia, and says, "I have a feeling strawberry is your flavor. Let's go in and sit for a moment." He holds the door for her as she sets eyes on a corner booth. To make her more comfortable, he inches the table closer to his side. Turns out, they fit perfectly together, Georgia taking up exactly as much space as the man gives away.

When the waitress arrives, she doesn't miss a beat. "Well don't you two make a fine couple. What can I get you?" She pops her gum and pulls out a pen buried in her brunette bun. No one is the wiser that he is a stranger to Georgia; she doesn't even know his name. Seemingly, he couldn't care less.

"We'll share the Kitchen Sink Sundae, please." He points to a photo in the diner menu.

"You got it, honey. Good choice." She winks and swivels, leaving the lovebirds to wait, as he cups his hands over Georgia's resting on the table.

Before the Loss, Georgia had momentary surges like this, when her senses rose from the dead. Sometimes the baby's wailing shocked her back to life. On the seldom mornings she mustered enough energy to rise from bed, she would wipe her eyes surprised to find a full sink of crusty dishes and spiders nesting in corners. If the fog lifted long enough, she plugged the sink, ran warm soapy water over the dishes, stopped it in time so the water wouldn't run over, and let them soak. She sprayed cleaner across the counter to kill trails of ants and watched them scramble to death before wiping them into her palm and sprinkling them like pepper into the trash. She tied the bulging trash bag at the top, pulled it loose from the can, and set it outside the front door of the apartment to take to the dumpster on the way out, with high hopes of making it that far.

Then, sitting with this man, she thinks back to the day of the Loss. How she'd found a sign written in her own handwriting, duct-taped to the front door of their apartment reminding her, *It was your birthday*. The depression made her lose time, so she'd taken to leaving herself reminders of what she might miss. She flipped on the only lamp in the room propped on a stack of neglected books including titles like *Love Does* and *Love Wins*, yellow and wrinkled. Georgia followed the ripe stench of her daughter's dirty diaper to the baby's crib where the girl whimpered. Above the baby, a wall calendar hung alongside another reminder. This one in permanent marker written directly on the wall in her own childlike cursive, *Stop being a shitty mother. Put the food down and take a walk*. She flipped from September to the next page of the calendar, ran her finger across the first row, and tapped on October 10. In the box, a sticky note was posted, *Now is the time*.

She stared at the child in her crib. The baby began to cry. Georgia lifted her, outstretched, then cradled her on her hip, more like a chimp than a child. While holding the child around the waist with one arm, she pushed the clunky old vacuum with the other, bouncing the child against her thigh to calm her. But the child only howled harder and harder, fighting with the roar of the vacuum—a cyclone of sound like thunder—crack.

Yank. Vacuum cord from the wall. Georgia sat the child on the floor, snot bubbling from her nose. At the top of each agonizing sob, she gagged, tiny cheeks blotched and veiny like the nose of a drunk. The mother began to panic when the child's nerves twitched and her fingers and toes stretched into webs. Circling the diapered girl on the carpet, Georgia broke into a sticky sweat. She ripped through her own hair with a brush, pulling it back at the nape. Fanning her face, Georgia paced. "Hush, baby. No more crying, baby. Mommy's here, baby." Begging, "Please, baby." When silence hit, Georgia thought it was over but as soon as the girl caught her breath another wave of anguish broke, like a strong tow pulling the mother under until Georgia was drowning. "Baby, baby, stop your crying, please, baby, please, please." Georgia thrashed through the apartment, a tornado unearthing anything soft and freestanding so as not to directly hurt the child, unbreakables bounced off walls, pillows and forks and books and toys, windows yanked open, doors slammed shut, until all her hard housework was undone, until she stood, huffing and puffing, over the girl.

Stop being a shitty mother. Put the food down and take a walk. Now is the time.

She never told Frank, she was simply following the signs.

The waitress arrives with a tray balanced above her shoulder. On top, a Neapolitan heap drenched in chocolate sauce with a cloud of whipped cream floating on two big bananas and double cherries on top, all heaped in a mini metal kitchen sink complete with little pipes as feet, tiny handles that really turn, and a faucet as big as Georgia's thumb. Two spoons balance on the basin's edges, one handle pointing toward Georgia, the other toward the man. He reaches around to Georgia's side and balances her spoon between his fingers. He plunges through the creamy top layer gathering every flavor, slices through the banana, and scoops up a maraschino at the end for an Olympic gold landing. Georgia applauds; her ocean eyes narrow toward her nose, crossing at the luscious spoonful. Georgia's dimples twitch, and she opens in slow motion. His face flushes, his hand wobbles, a bumpy ride to Georgia's lips, leaving a dot of whipped cream like a cloud at the tip of her nose.

"Oops, sorry for the turbulence." He chuckles and sets the spoon down on her side of the sink, holding the napkin he's lifted from his lap toward her.

Sugar pangs Georgia's jaw as she rolls the slick banana around like a snowball gathering cream until her tongue numbs and teeth ache. She tightens her eyes to savor the moment. It's clear to Georgia that he is sweet on her, a foreign sensation since the Loss. This man's offer is tempting, Georgia must admit. Tempting, quite like his shop offerings: a blue light special, a bargain of attention, prices slashed so low, for a moment, Georgia thinks she can find a need for it, wonders if she can pass it up. For the first time since the Gaining began, she wonders if she should stop the suffering. She opens her eyes just as the last morsel melts away, and pulls her hands out from under his.

"What's wrong?"

"I don't even know your name."

"You haven't asked."

"I don't think I want to know," she admits.

"Let's just finish our sundae. If you change your mind, just say the word."

It appears as if nothing seems to bother him, and Georgia considers this further proof that his offerings are bottom of the barrel. Georgia sets her spoon down. "I didn't always look like this," she says.

"No? How were you before?"

"Easier on the eyes."

"I could watch you all day, no sweat."

"That's not possible. I *know* how people see me."

"Maybe you only *think* you know. People are like puzzles. They're meant to be confusing. In the end, it's just a guessing game that puts all the pieces together."

"I wasn't expecting this." Georgia softens. They watch as the sundae turns soupy toward the sink's drain.

"Who could expect this?" he asks softly. "Such a surprise." His gaze turns inward. "Small surprises seem bigger in a life like mine," he says finally.

"What kind of life is that?"

"I keep things simple."

"*I am not simple,*" she says.

"That much I already know. I can see it in your eyes," he says.

He pays the bill, extending perfect courtesies to the waitress, hostess, cooks, patrons, and anyone else forgotten on their way out. As they resume their walk, she considers telling him how once upon a time, in a faraway land, there was a fork in the road. Back in a time before the Loss, before the Gaining, somewhere in between. How she knew that *Now is the time* because her calendar said October 10. How she had a plan to get a handle on her life again. How she cleaned the apartment for the first time in days while her daughter slept soundly on the bed, face up, to reduce risk. How for once she thought she felt a little better. But then her daughter woke and began to wail, and Georgia's flow was disrupted. The mother didn't have the right answers, she didn't know how to stop the baby's crying, how to ease the child from suffering. Offering her baby to the sea was how the mother could *save* her. And now this man sits before her. She has the strongest sense that he can somehow guard her, that he can somehow soothe her.

"So tell me, mister, what *is* your name?" she asks.

"Gabriel," he says. "Gabe Wade."

"Gabriel Wade. Well, it was nice to meet you. Lovely, really," Georgia says, unthreading her arm from Gabe's elbow. "This is our final destination."

"So soon?"

The truth is stuck in Georgia's throat like a tiny fish bone. She swallows hard to cram it down and steps away.

"I'm afraid so," she says.

The woman stands at a distance, not guessing how much she has come to matter to him already, that this loss is enough to mangle him. But he takes it with a kind generosity, with grace. Nods his head. In that moment, he reminds her of when she first began to recognize that empty space where Frank's freedom and her isolation meet. The space where some couples hold hands. It's as if he, like Georgia, is resigned to being left behind. She notices the slump of his shoulders as his shadow leads him away.

Perhaps it's his chivalry, coating her insides like syrup that moves her forward. Toward the coast. It occurs to her how late she is, maybe Frank will wonder, but the ocean's breadth charms her. Deep pummels of sound, then a gradual hush after each wave draws her closer to the edge.

The slanted route to Baby Beach hasn't changed much since the Loss, but she sees more than back then, when *Now is the time*. October

10. Now, with no child in hand, Georgia's able to take her shoes off and carry them. She looks beyond her feet, kicks a pebble with her bare toe. She watches it roll downhill past a mother jogging behind a fancy stroller, pushing the baby's chariot with such lightness and grace, Georgia swears she sees a smile on that mother's face. Georgia can't fathom it, a grin in the face of gravity, but sure enough, as they pass each other, the beaming mother's sweat smells like sweet perfume, her baby coos a light birdsong in tune with the mother's swift breath. Georgia squints at the shining town, looks around as if for the first time, specks of sunshine glitter off streetlights made to look like old-fashioned lanterns. A castle hovers over the edge of a high cliff in the distance, just one speckle against identical others, strewn together across rocky hills along the coast. It stretches out endless before her, nothing new, just that sameness. Her stomach turns like it did at the drain of the Kitchen Sink Sundae with Gabe. Strappy palm trees bend top-heavy, sprouting from surrounding crags, suspended, like a trick. Threadbare skies hardly hold together, wisps of pastels beaten frothy then smeared across a hard blue canvas. There's something about the way natural light absorbs into the lamppost; how the ancient masonry suddenly seems pristine; and the way the glib mother glides by her, that fills her with the feeling that none of it, *none of it*, is real.

Above the castle, Georgia spots a bright pink helium balloon loosed above the glossy snow globe town. As the balloon dwindles to a pin dot, Georgia inflates—brims to the thin rim of this fragile world. She rubs her eyes, thinks she's seeing things wrong, but there's no denying the rift of endless sea where land stops short at the shoreline. Baby Beach. Georgia opens her eyes. She searches the sea space for some sign of punishment—nothing. Just the constant sway of newborn waves mothered by the great expanse of sea. One single sound, the hiss of a sigh, is released in her outbreath, as she heaves her weight, leaving footprints on the beach erased slower than she can walk away.

Hours later than expected, when Georgia finally enters the bar, she finds Frank in the middle of the dance floor, drunk and slumped around a pretty young woman, slurring to a sappy jukebox song by the Boss, Frank's favorite. Georgia pries him off the young miss, tossing Frank's arm around her shoulder to carry him home. On the way back, they pass Gabriel's shop and in the dim recesses, she sees he's sweeping out the far corner of the showroom. Georgia drags Frank up the weathered wooden stairs to their second-floor seaside apartment. When they reach the top, she says she could've used a second man for the job. She unlocks the door with Frank's keys, sets them on the hook beside the door, and dumps him on the bed.

Before disrobing, Georgia takes a moment to stand on the porch, to breathe fresh air under the moon. On the porch railing, she notices a lifeless monarch. *Left behind*, she thinks and pinches its dead wings in her fingers, holds it up to the moonlight, and lets go. The majesty helicopters, swirled in gentle Pacific winds, landing on the ground below just after Georgia steps inside. In front of the small safe gathering dust in the corner, she opens the latch with one hand, unties the bright pink silk bow at her crown with the other. Carefully, she coils the scarf in her palm, places it dead center in the middle of the empty safe. She locks it up—fireproof and airtight—sheds her clothes, and climbs naked into her bed next to Frank.

You—& My Abstract Theory of You

R. J. Keeler

Ah, the gradation of the curve of her torso near midriff,
her swaged hair blunted dark and streaked with platinum.
Metafluids surge molten, flattening our unequal seas;
nothing escapes her tight event horizon.

My theory of you, dear—way abstract for simple calculus.
I'll re-invent higher-order operators to factor your figures,
to synch to the intricate chambers of your catenary heart.
Onward I sail to plunge back into *reductio ad absurdum*.

The star map of your inner spinors—what heavenly body,
pixelated by shafts of collider energy, jolts of chromos.
It always makes my toes curl up and sigh, to so wish
integration to your hot, under-hood, combustion engine.

You, Lamborghini to my worn-out Citroën, race down
the speedway lapping and lapping me, again and again.
How can you be so fast, so driven? May I now please
slide down this hyperbolic to your magnetic monopole?

You—exactly like some racy Horsehead Nebula,
birthplace of hot new suns, of breaking all limits.
We intersect our divisions, battle for summation,
field big-bang oscillations, continuous space warps.

There is no theory, useful or known, to explain
why your clandestine agencies hold me in line.
Or what love really means, or decipher your factors.
Your prime integer ever signs my lonesome heart.

Please allow me to disentangle your q-bits.

Carnage

Soraya Safavid

> *Give me my wife Michal whom I betrothed to*
> *myself for a hundred foreskins of the Philistines.*

I'm no woman
when you send for me, when you tear me
out of the ground—

No matter that my limbs end
in feet or that my trunk
doesn't root down in dirt.

Fourteen years I grew hard
against your hands and the things
you once did with a mouth.

On the road to your house
dust thickens my blood
to honey—it is savage

what it asks the heart to do,
to shove such thickness
through the limbs.

Don't think because I say honey
I mean sweetness.
What sweetness I stored

you sapped from me. In my veins
the names of your five wives
harden to amber.

Stripped
of shade—no bird's joy—
the broom you used

to sweep off the dirt of the herds
then discarded. The stink of sheep
still clings to your skin

when your hand yokes
my throat, the one you used
to stroke the strings.

The other one
that smells like gore
hangs at your side—

Hand that killed
one hundred men then killed
one hundred more

than my father asked for
and flung the bloody
skins at his feet.

So, why the bad math
when you retrieve me?
Has the man who always numbered

everything he thought was his—sheep
stones. songs. soldiers—forgotten
how to count? Or is this desire

to show me I'm worth
half the price
your hand once paid to hold me?

Hand you harness to my hip
now that it's night and my father's
dead and headless—

When the one he gave me to,
after you bailed, wept *Michal*,
Michal behind me all the way to Bahurim.

When no one can watch
the bristle and flinch
while you finger the ditch

where my breath ends
then fence my face
in your hands. My body splinters

in a kiss that feels like carnage—
payment in meat
as tribute—levied against my mouth—

And still, you refuse to say my name.
Michal. Less tag than ax
my father buried in the stump

of my body as a question—*Who is like God?*
Survey you evade in your hunger
to consume the remains of my father.

Your incinerating kiss
not indifference to the asking
but fear of the answer. Michal,

meaning also *brook, stream*
holding only a little water.
Not unlike what exits my eyes.

Mouth in flames, I breathe
my name back into you—
Who is like God, David?

until I am ash in your arms—Don't
mistake me. Not
the char that remains

after the fire. But the tree—
bald, blackened—
that survives the burning.

What I Took from the River

Anja Semanco

I DROVE DOWN THE WINDING ROADS OF YOSEMITE NATIONAL PARK IN A WHITE fifteen-seater van, the open windows whipping strands of unwashed hair into my face. I sat high off the pavement in that rattling rented Chevy, bouncing like a pinball with every bump in the road.

Yosemite Valley cupped me then in the stone palms of her hands as the van descended. In those swells and curves, I saw something familiarly feminine. A matriarchal relief. I don't know what the men sitting next to me saw.

There were four of us that afternoon, me and three coworkers who had quickly become dear friends. It was the end of a four-day retreat hosted in Yosemite with some of the country's greatest outdoor athletes. I was most certainly not one of them. I was a mere assistant to the executive director, the newest hire at an organization that I thought at the time was to become my dream job. I wore an exuberant exterior while saying over and over again, "I'm just so grateful to be here," to everyone I met.

The athletes were the spokespeople for climate change, the brilliant recognizable faces of commitment to a cause. The rest of us were mere organizers. We clung behind the scenes putting the framework together hoping their influence and accomplishments could inspire change.

Though other women were invited to this retreat and wandered around the campsite in joyful groups, I felt that we had just concluded a long stretch of days of men talking. And talking. And talking. Already the dream job facade was cracking. I put myself to sleep reading Mary Oliver poems alone in my tent while the men discussed any sort of topic long into the night. Maybe they solved climate change with all that talking—the reason they'd gathered in Yosemite in the first place—while I dreamed of birds. But three years have passed and I still haven't seen them come up with anything worthwhile.

That final afternoon though, we had a glorious stretch of several hours in which the athletes headed home and the executive director disappeared to climb some rock face with a big wig from Aspen Ski Company. We were free to wander unobserved. And while I put on a good face for the four days of men speaking at their trapped audience, in this stretch of hours between obligations, I reveled in the sweet feminine silence.

Some team members headed out to Reno to catch their flights back to Colorado, but the rest of us had flights the next morning out of San Francisco. The four of us decided to spend the handful of hours remaining in Yosemite swimming in the Merced River.

I scanned the various pull-offs along the shoulder of the road for twenty minutes as we curled down the mountain before spotting a perfect van-sized space near the river's edge. My friends unbuckled before I'd even put the van in park. They flung open the doors, stripped down to boxers, and ran to the water.

Alone at the van, I squirmed into a damp swimsuit yanked over sweaty skin, only partially concealed from passing traffic by the open van door. My legs were sticky and wrinkled from four days without a shower. I traced the bumps and lines with my fingers, those small mountains and rivers of my own. Then I wrapped myself in a camp towel and in bare feet followed the boys to the river.

JOHN THE BAPTIST PLUNGED Jesus into the Jordan River and it was, well, baptism. John Muir—that continuing problematic character—had to take it a step further saying, "Heaven knows that John the Baptist was not more eager to get all his fellow sinners into the Jordan than I to baptize all of mine in the beauty of God's mountains." And so the infernal measuring contest between men was underway.

In 1880 Muir married Louisa Strentzel and brought her to Yosemite. I imagine he expected to have a long and happy marriage, so it must have been especially disappointing when Louisa's fear of bears and trouble climbing at Muir's pace made her first trip to Yosemite her last. She never returned to the "beauty of God's mountains" again.

At the time, I couldn't know if my first trip to Yosemite would be my last. I didn't imagine it would be, though I craved to return and experience that place without all the posturing around the campfire every night. I don't doubt Louisa's fear of bears—my own fear has kept me wary of grizzly country for a long time—but made to keep pace with Muir and his ego, I probably would not have wanted to return in that way either. Despite our 140-year gap in history, I felt a deep connection with Louisa.

I've often wondered, made to keep pace with only myself, what other opportunities I may have had in life. Rather than falling in love with people or landscapes in the slow and attentive way I prefer, I have so often been forcibly baptized in them instead—often by men.

How different could Louisa's life have been? How different could mine still be? I have fantasized about what it would be like to take Louisa by the hand and tenderly introduce her to that valley in the ways her husband couldn't. I'd let Johnny disappear into the hills at his insufferable, competitive pace, while Louisa and I waded bare-skinned into the Merced. Perhaps we'd spot a bear lumbering down to the water's edge, the Greek goddess Artemis, priestess and protectress of the Pole Star helping us overcome any fear. We'd be baptized then not by Muir, or even God's mountains, but rather by the ruler of the cosmos herself.

AFTER FLASHING ONLY A handful of passing cars, I made my way down to the river where my friends were already in the water.

Jake was on the far shore, climbing up over one rock, then another. It took him only moments before he summited a stout stone cliff about ten feet above the river. He was preparing to jump when he suddenly shouted to the three of us onshore.

"Hey! There's money down there!" He pointed into the body of the river. We all looked up then.

"Like a wishing well?" I shouted back over the hum of the river, assuming he'd found a few coins tossed by hikers.

"No, a bunch of paper money," he said. And with that, he jumped off the cliff, plunged into the water, but came up empty-handed. He swam back to the group and settled on a rock. The four of us gazed at the shaded pool.

"Seriously," he said. "There's money at the bottom."

"We should go after it," I said after a moment's pause.

"Kind of seems like a trap, doesn't it?" said Justin. "Like there might be a river witch at the bottom who holds you down."

We laughed at this but couldn't help but stare at the rippling surface of the water. I waded to the tops of my knees, immediately filled with the chill of the snowmelt river. I looked back.

"Should we do it?" I asked. There was a moment of hesitation. Then, with a loud splash, Joe ran ahead and jumped into the water. He swam quickly to the dark pool, climbed the cliff, and stared down.

"There's definitely money over here," he shouted back.

After days listening to the adventurous, if overbearing stories of men, I wanted one of my own. I jumped into the water too. The cold pummeled my chest as I swam to where Joe pointed from above. I looked down into the clear cold river, filled my lungs with air, and dove.

IN SLAVIC MYTHOLOGY, DROWNING is rarely an accident. A riverbank is not often just a riverbank. And pale, naked, pupil-less women dangling from the willows are not to be trusted, no matter how sweetly they call you.

The *rusalki* are a mythic river spirit—the water women who fertilize the crops each spring, bringing the floods over the banks of the river and into the fields. It is possible, perhaps even likely, that before the onslaught of Christianity tainted the ideologies of these land-worshipping people, the *rusalki* were beloved—even worshipped. It is possible that women, with an obvious maternity line (while paternity could remain uncertain), led their households and communities.

These delightful fertility goddesses who brought fecundity to the community were later vilified by Christians as "unclean" gods. This supreme creator deteriorated to at best a murderess, and at worst a villainous river whore.

Rusalki by this telling are not beings born from the underworld but are rather mortal women transformed by it. A *rusalka* is said to be the result of any woman who dies a "bad" death. A "bad" death being violent, often at the hands of an angry man, or self-inflicted upon learning of a husband's infidelity. Most notably, a "bad" death occurred when a woman died before she had the chance to give birth. These liminal women dying bad deaths dwell in the rivers and nearby trees for all of eternity, luring men to their watery deaths. If the *rusalki* can drown their unfaithful lover, or find themselves baptized in the spirit of Christ, only then can they be freed to an afterlife.

I quite like these river women instilling fear in the hearts of men. I like the way they are almost never depicted alone, but rather in groups as sisters, laughing together. Their dualistic nature between the land of the living and the land of the dead is ripe with the symbolism of the unconscious, the other world, and the cyclical nature of life, death, and life again.

I like to imagine *rusalki* lurking in the shaded pools of the Merced, their white teeth gleaming.

MY EYES BLURRED IN the cold river water. The shadows from the cliffs were blinding. As I reached a hand toward a pale, oblong shape on the bottom of the river, I was suddenly filled with fear. My hand grazed the edge of a pile of slimy leaves that curled around my fingers. I panicked, kicking my body back to the surface.

"I think they're just rocks," I shouted back to the bank. I hovered over the unknown objects, aggressively trying to catch my breath in the freezing water.

"No," said Jake, shaking his head. "It's definitely money."

Joe looked down over the cliff to where I floated. "I do think it's money," he said.

So I dove again. I kicked wildly to the bottom, reached out my hand, and frantically grasped at the sand. Something fluttered in my clenched fist. I broke the surface and looked into my palm.

"I got a twenty!" I shouted.

Immediately, the boys dove into the water. I felt a rush, holding that $20 bill between my fingers. For the next hour, we took turns swimming to the bottom. The twenty was the largest bill we found and I was rightfully smug about it. On my second dive, I retrieved a $10 bill. The others found ones and a five. After several trips down, only one bill remained tucked into the river bottom with $37 recovered between the four of us.

As we swam over the last dollar, the boys excitedly told me a myth about a plane full of cocaine and drug money crashing somewhere in Yosemite a bunch of years ago. The story, they said, was that the cargo drifted into the river. They only half-jokingly wondered if the money at the bottom of the river was a remnant of drug money from the crash.

This story is not a myth at all, it turns out, but the boys' telling of it isn't quite right either. In 1977, in the middle of winter, an American plane loaded with 6,000 pounds of marijuana bales (not cocaine) did crash into Lower Merced Pass Lake, spilling its cargo along with 1,500 gallons of aviation fuel and hydraulic fluid.

Despite park rangers' and law enforcements' best attempts, they couldn't recover much from the thickly frozen lake. Among Yosemite climbers, word spread like wildfire about "Dope Lake," and it wasn't long before joints sparking with aviation fluid were springing up in Camp 4—a rowdy climbers' basecamp. It wasn't until June 1977 that the fuselage and cargo were fully recovered from the lake, by which time thousands of pounds of weed had walked off.

Actually, this telling might not be quite right either. The film *Valley Uprising* depicts a slightly different version in which climbers discovered the plane crash well before rangers or other law enforcement. One of the climbers said that even the rangers didn't discover the plane crash until the weed was "all gone." He said this with such a self-satisfied grin that I cringed watching the footage.

Later, in an interview with NPR titled "Lake Chronicopia," Dale Bard, an early Yosemite climber, explained to interviewer Julia Dewitt how law enforcement culminated in Yosemite National Park as climbers set up illegal camps and butted heads with park rangers in the classic and clumsy tale of peace and love versus authority.

During the interview, Bard explained that the park service wanted to make an example of him and kicked him out of Yosemite National Park for ninety days. He stayed in the park anyway, drying sheets of weed pulled from the lake out in a hidden field. Dewitt asked why he didn't just leave for a couple of months, given the risk. "I mean, that is a long time," Bard said. "And it's too long of a time. If you're used to climbing every day, that's not an option."

During *Valley Uprising*, another of the climbers said with frustration that the reaction from rangers was unreasonable. Climbers, he said, "were using the park for its intended use," unlike everyone else who came to visit or perhaps unlike the dispossessed California Natives booted from their land.

In all the coverage I found, it sounded like a lot of men endlessly talking.

IN THE *DIVINE COMEDY*, Dante observed sinners reaching the Garden of Eden at the top of Mount Purgatory where they were baptized in the river Lethe to forget their sins, then drank from the river Eunoe to strengthen the memories of their goodness and complete their purgatorial journey.

I am reminded of this in reflecting on the legacy of Yosemite and the Sierra's colonization. I am reminded of it when I think of my bookshelves once lined with heavily dog-eared collections of Muir's essays. And the hours of my life I've willingly given away watching films like *Free Solo*, *Valley Uprising*, and the so painfully titled *Ode to Muir* that the tediously white male–dominated outdoor industry has carefully funneled my way. All of these monoliths forgot their sins, then strengthened only the memories of their goodness.

I no longer wish to be baptized by Muir.

I couldn't find any information about drug money as part of the plane's cargo, but Lower Merced Pass Lake is only about three miles as the crow flies from where we were swimming. It might be tempting to believe the bills on the bottom of the river were the tailings of that white, masculine fairy tale. When I think back on it now, I'm much more inclined to invoke the myth of the *rusalki*. Though far from their Eastern European home, luring us to the river bottom with the thin promise of riches seems like the type of antics these wild women would employ. I wonder now if the *rusalki* were calling me home.

AFTER AN HOUR IN the river, I was shaking with cold, my sinuses full of freezing water. My gums ached and my teeth were screaming from chilled jawbones. I slid my face into the water one last time and saw nothing but darkness swirling below. I swam instead to a rock and sat with my body half-exposed in the breezy afternoon air. I felt my face paling and my lips turning blue as I watched the others make their final dives.

When they came up empty-handed for the third time, I swam to the other shore and laid my bare belly on a hot, dry rock. No matter how many times they jumped into the water, they couldn't salvage the final bill.

Somewhere beneath the water, a congregation of women grinned.

WHEN WE FINALLY MET back up with our executive director in the late afternoon, the four of us excitedly recounted our story, waving our damp bills for him to examine.

"Interesting," he said in the same way you might tell a toddler the rock they found in the driveway was interesting. As I drove us out of the park and onto the darkening highway, he regaled us with the heroic tale of his climb, pausing only to tell me, again and again, to slow down. A month or two later, the Aspen Ski Company director published a story of their climb—how they almost didn't make it, then at the final moment, overcame the wall. I think it was meant to inspire people to take action on climate change, but all I heard was a bunch of men talking.

Of Lavender and Mint

Phyn Vermin

I once cried gentle tears
in mourning of certainty
for I seem to have lost my way

The path, once clear
was overgrown with brambles
and tangled oaks that stretched
hanging limbs across the way
They spoke to me in an old tongue;
"You may not pass here."

But there in the thicket,
bound in a harness of thorns,
but so, too, hints
of lavender and mint,
I found you.

I was haughty at the start,
sure-footed over tended trail,
fresh boots upon my feet
and rations planned for days of trek

When the roads became shadowed
under canopies of flora I could not name,
I forged ahead still; nubile confidence
gifted only naive youth
I was certain of my map
I listened not
to the whispering wood

"If you listen closer,"
you said, through my tears,
"they are telling you where to turn."

But all I could see
was the blood, crisp on your skin
Black clots where thorns buried deep
I dug through my bag; I had prepared for this
But fresh cleaned wounds bleed like berries,
and thorns in flesh
are not so easily
forgotten

Once free, you held my hand;
"If you listen, they know the path."
But I could hear nothing
past the scent
of lavender
and mint.

I lost my map, but not the quest
as you galloped with me down trails
unmarked, unkempt, unknown
I came to know my body
and yours
as the animals do,
fire under skin,
and nightly,
tracing scars like constellations
left behind so long ago

And all along you were teaching me
to listen for the song
in a language I was born for,
but had forgotten along the way

I traveled with you til
my boots peeled off my feet
and I could feel every jagged pebble,
every sharp blade of grass,

every slimy, moss-engulfed stone,
across my soles
I traveled with you til
I learned how to read
the music of the forest
with my toes

When the rabbit crossed my path
and tumbled over the cliffside,
head over feet,
fractured skull over shattered pelvis,
I followed it down,
for I heard in that moment
that old tongue whispering to me,
"Now you must leap."

We lost sight of each other there
but I had not lost the scent
of lavender and mint.

My clothes rotted off long ago,
since replaced by deer and vine
My bag now lost too,
replaced with fur satchel
In it now, just bones
that rattle as I travel,
telling stories I'd forgotten
until now

The forest feeds me daily
as I follow no trail,
just this journey
to the source
of lavender and mint.

Abduction

Tyler Wells Lynch

THE FIRST TIME MEREDITH SANGER WAS ABDUCTED SHE HAD DRIVEN THE Windstar out to the desert to ask God if a six-burner gas grill is worth $900. Alphonse said it was essential. He required the virile perks of an all-beef diet to finish building the deck, which had idled in the summer months as a stratum of wobbly joists. What worried Meredith more than her husband's laziness was how their daughter Rachel, in her blooming adolescence, had taken to prancing across the beams, miming the Barbie of Swan Lake. A broken bone was out of the question. Every bill was on the calendar. There were only so many hours in the work week, and as much as Meredith would like to eat healthier, barbecue ribs seemed the price of her daughter's safety. So, brewing with the anxiety Doctor Ramirez said was just gas, Meredith braved the pinched sciatic nerve that made kneeling such a chore and knelt before a crop of sandstone in the Tehachapi foothills, hoping to speak with God.

His voice flowed from the mouth of an ashy chuckwalla, who revealed through vacant sockets that there is wisdom in abiding the will of thy husband. *It is the mandate of my children*, she thought she heard Him say, *to consume the flesh of the cloven-footed beasts, for they are delicious*. The tiny reptile bore the thinnest of smiles as it spoke, lit by a column of moonlight Meredith welcomed as His divine presence. But it was still only dusk. The moon, only a fingernail sliver, had barely crested the mountains to the south. To the west, sunlight still painted the Arvin apple orchards, casting lanky shadows and petting the air with a rosy aroma. But the light that fell here, decorating the chuckwalla in ashen stubble, was fluorescent and milky.

Meredith looked up to see a disk-shaped object hovering in perfect silence. Smooth and shiny with no clear bolts or couplings, it reminded Meredith of the Mikasa dinnerware set she bought at the Big Lots in Bakersfield. Filigreed suspicions of some ancient language ran round the edge of the disk, resembling Greek or Aramaic—or was it Thai? She knew her Old Testament. She had read the *Pistis Sophia*, whose feminine emanation birthed the tetragrammaton: *Yhwh himself.* She had read, mesmerized, about Ezekiel's cherub, whose form resembled eye-dappled wheels the color of beryl stone, all traveling to and from and within and embodying the living creatures of the world, the wisdom of the eternal. She felt their presence, here, as a blinding light, through which Meredith began to levitate and wish she hadn't eaten that tuna melt. Cheese gave her gas. The Windstar's fuel light had blinked on at the Big Lots in Bakersfield. Nine hundred dollars was a lot of money for a grill. She didn't know how to cook ribs. And Rachel was probably allergic to honey.

"Can you dim the lights?" Meredith asked, feeling the sensation of moving indoors, somewhere warm. But even here, in what she assumed was the nave of divinity, she was fixed on the pain in her back. For three weeks she'd been pressing her boss at the fulfillment center for a new chair, and for three weeks she'd received empty promises and worsening pain. Fewer shifts were not an option. She would miss her numbers and, with it, her half of the family pie, her share of the health insurance she and Alphonse received separately, lest they incur the expense of another dependent. Every night she prayed for relief, but on this night, the night He chose to answer her, she had prayed for shopping advice.

She found herself on a gurney in a circular green room, not unlike the padded cells she'd seen in scary movies that made her want to hug her daughter. Always one to spurn the doting of her embarrassing parents, Rachel would wiggle away and insist they just watch the movie already. "It's too scary for an eleven-year-old," Meredith would say, to which Rachel would insist she's not a girl anymore.

Some minutes passed in the green room. Maybe hours. She looked for signs of time's passage—blotches of mildew, cracked paint, the stench of old wood like all the homes she'd ever lived in—but found only a sterile antechamber. It was so quiet she could hear the vessels in her head flowing with the matter of her thoughts. But maybe this wasn't real. Maybe she was dreaming. Maybe she was dead. She pinched her forearm. The pain reminded her of the time Alphonse had to distract her while Dr. Ramirez administered a tetanus boost. Another nail had emerged from the floorboards in the kitchen, risen like stones from eroded centuries, and it would surprise no one that Meredith was the one to suffer its return. She had that kind of luck. Like Job. It was not out of the question that her life, too, was forfeit.

They appeared as men in gray coats—or were they women?—materializing like angels—the haloed ones with white frocks, not the winged seraphs with eyes like a spider. How long had they been there? Their skin was smooth and leathery, their eyes large and vacant like goggles on an old-timey gas mask. A rising dread coursed through Meredith's veins. As she motioned to rise she found her legs were still. Frozen. She couldn't move. The stirrings of a panic attack—the jittery, heart-racing death taunt—oozed to the surface and ate the light.

"Where am I?" she panted. "Is this Epcot?"

A voice like a dying radio station said, "We ask you tell us of the music man. Miles Davis. He who is I am. The sound of a word. His breath. We ask of it."

"What? Miles David?" Meredith quit tugging and a jolt of pain shot up her leg, the return of her sciatica. "Ugh! Lord, let me enter your kingdom with the spine of Samson."

"This is not the kingdom of heaven," one of the beings said, only it had no mouth to move.

"Is it purgatory? Am I in purgatory?" She thought of the time Alphonse got the family kicked out of *Mission: Space* for sneaking nips of Old Grand-Dad. "Please, Lord, banish this pain!"

Somewhere a light flickered. As it did, Meredith's stress fell away like leaves and the pain in her back exhaled, dissipated.

"Oh, sweet relief," she said.

"We must know when is Miles Davis," the beings continued. "He who is I am."

"Tell us about music," the other one said. "How it behaves."

"And surfing. Tell us of these time sports."

She remembered nothing more.

THAT SUNDAY, ALPHONSE WOULD enter church for the first time without his wife. She was missing, had been for almost two days, the Windstar discovered out in the desert by the Arvin apple orchards. The gas tank had been empty, which to Alphonse seemed a reason for hope as much as despair. Had she finally lost her beak and wandered off into the desert to become buzzard food? Or had she been abducted by some crazed killer with a three-part name? Alphonse kicked himself for not taking seriously the concerns of her daughter. Rachel had wanted to call the police as soon as the sun went down Friday, hardly an hour after Meredith left to buy some Advil.

"She probably got distracted in the home goods section," Alphonse had said. "She'll come back with a new pepper shaker and a pillow that says *Hope*."

"No, Dad. She's missing," Rachel said, to which Alphonse, again, waved her away so he could watch his *CSI*. They didn't call 911 until midnight, at which point who knows how many precious hours they'd lost? It was his complacency. He knew it. He didn't need Rachel to remind him.

They didn't sleep that night, although they tried in the early morning hours, after the police had left. As the sun rose, casting Venetian shadows across the bed, Alphonse was woken by the trail of Rachel's voice, lilting through sniffly breaths, "What if she left us?"

Alphonse took a moment to orient himself. *It's Saturday morning. Only one night in the belly of the whale.* "She would never leave you," he said.

"And you?" Rachel said.

"Of course not, Rae. I would never leave you—*we* would never leave you."

"No," Rachel said, wiping away tears. "Would she ever leave *you*?"

The next day Alphonse and Rachel printed eighty-six missing person signs using an unflattering photo of Meredith holding a plate of microwave nachos. Streaks of faded toner lanced the nachos and Meredith's face, making her look jaundiced. A detective named Árbenz promised to keep the family abreast. She and some others were working on a forensic profile of the Windstar and would know soon enough if anyone but family members had been in the vehicle. "I've seen this before," Árbenz said. "People wander off when life takes a turn. I guess the desert's a nice place to file your thoughts. Not sure why. Seems a cruel and unforgiving place to me, but that's what those turquoise-wearing dingbats say. They mean well. I knew a guy from Eureka once drove out to the desert, came back with a face tattoo he didn't remember getting."

"That's not my wife," Alphonse said. "She would never get a tattoo. She would never leave without telling us. She has an anxiety disorder and would never put herself in danger like that."

"Well, *how much do we really know anyone?* is something my mother used to say when we asked what's for dinner. Point is, someone you know is only someone you know until they're someone else."

"That doesn't help," Rachel said. "My mom's missing and that doesn't help."

"Of course not. Look at me. Smart girl. I guess I'll be off. Any evidence is good evidence, is the moral here, and we'll find some evidence when the lab report on that Windstar gets back. You can sleep on that."

Church friends came and went, all with tuna casseroles and baked ziti and beef stroganoff in ceramic dishes they insisted had no return date. They said there would be a vigil that night. At the church. Alphonse and Rachel should come and pray for Meredith's safe return, to which Rachel said of course and Alphonse, "Why not?" After all, these people had witnessed his marriage following the hasty move from Michigan, all to consecrate the child who had, sinfully, been born out of wedlock. It was a mess, and the congregants of Westminster Presbyterian, friendly as they were, had seen more of Alphonse's life than he cared to share. But Meredith wanted to be a part of the community, to host and attend potlucks in equal share. "We mustn't separate from the body," she would say, unwrapping some porcelain figurine.

In recent years, the Sanger home had fallen into such a state that even Alphonse was embarrassed to host people. The drywall in the kitchen was beginning to bow, but Rachel needed braces. The deck was an aging rack of two-by-tens, but Rachel needed glasses. The garage was overflowing with newspapers and VHS tapes, but Rachel needed an allergist. The last guest to visit the house was one of Rachel's friends, Cynthia, whose family also went to Westminster. One day, as they played together in Rachel's room, Alphonse overheard Cynthia ask, "Why does your house smell like a tool shed?" Rachel never asked to have friends over again after that.

The minister, Reverend Olson, had taken an interest in her, asking after her on Sundays when she opted to stay home. The excuse Meredith offered was that Rachel would be a teenager soon and teenagers needed to be alone sometimes. Alphonse knew Meredith never had any alone time as a kid, and he, too, cherished his solitude, so there was a balancing act to perform. It was a frequent topic on Sundays, one which Meredith raised after services had ended and the congregation had fled for the nearest Golden Corral. Reverend Olson, furrowing his brow and tilting his head, would quote Luke or Matthew, reminding Meredith that nothing is concealed that will not be revealed, nor hidden that will not be known. To this, Alphonse would dangle the car keys and say, "Jesus never had a daughter." Then he would laugh and make for the Windstar, which, for some reason, had a coin-operated kiddie ride sticking out of the trunk.

At the vigil, Reverend Olson asked Alphonse to say a few words. He was terrified of public speaking and knew his stammering and pregnant pauses would draw a dose of gossip he was loath to entertain, so he declined. In his place Meredith's friend Judith Peterson spoke, the mother of Rachel's friend Cynthia. She and Meredith had been calling each other besties ever since they discovered they were from the same small town in upstate New York, a place called Palmyra. They hadn't known each other growing up, but it was enough for them to pretend to like all the same things. Judith spoke of Meredith as if she'd known her since birth. She played up her charitable works, which included bake sales and a $3 monthly donation to the Red Cross. She talked about how strong Meredith was—even using the word "was"—and told a story about the time Meredith offered brownies as a halftime snack at their kids' soccer game, how she was surprised to be turned down by the fitness-focused coach. "She just wanted everyone to eat and be merry."

Reverend Olson told a story about the time he found Meredith asleep in the pew and had to wake her because her snoring was disturbing other congregants. Apparently, she had just finished a twelve-hour shift. Laughter and waterworks filled the church. To Alphonse, the whole thing felt like a funeral.

"We'll find her," Alphonse said, gripping Rachel's hand.

"Ouch, Dad. You're hurting my hand."

"Sorry, Rae Rae. I just want you to know, we'll find her, with or without these people."

Reverend Olson led the parishioners in Psalm 73, which was yet another bleak choice, given the circumstances. The only thing Alphonse enjoyed less than public speaking was public singing. Rachel, however, sounded lovely, so lovely that, for a moment, Alphonse wondered if her daughter might have a career in music.

The slam of the door in the narthex brought the singing to a stop. Alphonse saw the look in Reverend Olson's eyes and knew.

"Praise Jesus!" someone shouted.

Gasps filled the nave as Alphonse swung around to glimpse the figure of his wife standing between the pews, arms outstretched. Flocks of parishioners fell to their knees around her. She looked cold.

BY THE TIME DETECTIVE Árbenz arrived, Meredith had repeated her story twelve times without a chance to pee. Alphonse had been handing her glass after glass of water, and Reverend Olson, trying as he might to quell the gaggle of prying churchgoers, could not help but supply his own questions. Even Rachel looked more perplexed than relieved. *What happened? Where had she been? Why did she leave?* She'd already told them. She'd gone out to the desert. *Why?* To pray. *And?* And she was abducted. *By whom?* By God. *What did God look like?* There were two of them. *Two Gods?* That's what I said. *Blasphemy.* That's what I saw. *You didn't see God.* I saw Ezekiel's wheel, spinning like wheels the color of beryl stone. *What did He want?* To find Miles Davis. *You didn't see God.*

Detective Árbenz asked the same questions, although Meredith appreciated how indifferent she was. "These kinds of revelations happen all the time," the detective said. "Nothing to worry about. There's a new prophet every week out here."

"I'm not a prophet," Meredith said.

"Sure you're not. Now tell me about your comings and goings. How'd you get to church this morning?"

Meredith thought about it, searched for a more reassuring answer but could only offer the truth. "I don't know."

Everyone stared, waiting for Meredith to elaborate. She did not.

"Gotcha," Árbenz continued. "What's your last memory?"

Meredith clutched her belly. It was gurgling. "Standing over there, in the aisle, looking at my daughter and feeling cold."

Meredith thought she heard Reverend Olson sigh—or did someone pass gas? She watched the minister leave the assembly and disappear into the sacristy. *It must be lunch time*, Meredith thought. After a few more questions Alphonse took the detective aside. He was losing his temper, arguing that Meredith wasn't even sunburned after two days in the desert, which, the detective agreed, was both odd and true. But Árbenz just shrugged and said these things happen.

On the drive home, Meredith was grateful for the silence. They stopped at an In-N-Out Burger and ate in the car listening to talk radio. Apparently there were people coming from someplace else in search of someplace new, and the Kern County Fair opened Saturday. A giant sow named Brenda was on auction, and deep-fried Oreos were $2 a pop.

WORD GOT TO THE press that a devout Christian woman had been abducted by aliens. At least, that's how they interpreted her insistence that the little green men of popular culture were, in fact, dualistic manifestations of God. Almost overnight, Meredith assumed celebrity status among all the disciples of the esoteric. No sooner would she finish a call with a ufologist than another would begin with some paranormal researcher or ghost hunter or professional debunker. They would ask questions and listen without judgment, but the words they chose to print proved they had not, in fact, been listening. Each, without fail, had their own idea of what happened to Meredith, and none of them involved the truth. Even Alphonse and Rachel seemed uneasy with Meredith's testament. They avoided the subject, and when Meredith mentioned some new story or inquiry, they would glance at each other, waiting for the other to say something. Rachel broke the silence one night when she mentioned, over a dinner of green beans and chicken nuggets, that Cynthia Peterson thinks the Sanger family is a cult. Alphonse laughed and said, "At least cults know how to fleece a little cash from their followers. Mom's play is a longer con."

Meredith knew he'd meant it as a joke, but she couldn't help but huff and take her dinner into the other room. From then on she was selective about media inquiries and secretive about interviews. As a family, the Sangers stopped going to church, and in lieu of community worship, Meredith rose early on Sundays to pray beneath the morning sun, balancing her knees, miraculously without pain, on the wobbly deck joists that Alphonse hadn't touched since July. But as more weeks passed Alphonse grew more and more suspicious. One night, after a call with a reporter from the *Review-Journal*, Meredith found Alphonse standing in the doorway, blocking the exit. "Miles Davis?" he said.

"Apparently he's a trumpet player."

"I know he's a trumpet player. I know who Miles Davis is. What I don't know is why God or some space creature from Alpha Centaur or whatever would give a hoot about Miles Davis—much less why he would ask *you* about him."

"We've been over this, Alphonse. It's not for me to divine God's plan. I am only a messenger—and who said it was a *he*?"

"It just doesn't make sense. I mean, sympathize with me for a second. With your daughter. Put yourself in our shoes. Rachel's best friend won't even talk to her. They snicker behind our backs. We're ostriches in our community."

"*Ostracized*," Meredith corrected.

"How long is this gonna last?"

"Many times I've asked myself that same question," Meredith said, plowing past her husband in search of comfort cookies. "And many times I've prayed for His guidance. And without fail, He delivers. You should try it."

The next morning Meredith was laid off. Her manager said she'd failed to hit her quota, but she knew that was a lie. Even if she'd missed her numbers the policy was three strikes before you're fired and this would've been her second. It was the abduction. The press attention. The stigma of the thing. The furtive glances Meredith received when she left the fulfillment center said it all: *That woman's a galactic kook.*

Thinking only of a new set of numbers, worried how she would afford groceries next week, Meredith headed to Westminster to pray.

Inside, she knelt before the communion table and felt, for the first time since before the abduction, a shiver of pain shoot down her sciatic nerve. She prayed to find some image of the Lord like she'd seen in the desert, some guiding light that might reveal a path, but all she found was the gothic fascia and ornamental soffits of an empty church. What little sunlight penetrated the stained glass ran off the brass candelabras and crucifixes, streaking motes of dust in perpetual twilight. It was suffocating.

"I'd know that Windstar anywhere." Reverend Olson's voice echoed through the transept. He sounded feeble, as if recovering from the flu. "You don't see wood paneling on cars much these days. Something nostalgic about it."

Meredith took a seat in the front pew. "In a past life my husband was a handyman."

"But now?"

Meredith was struck by the look on the reverend's face. Gone were the warm smile and piercing green eyes, which once radiated love. He looked old. "But now he's tired and I can't blame him. The truth is such a heavy thing."

Reverend Olson took a seat next to Meredith and looked up at the ceiling. Meredith could smell alcohol on his breath. "They say in physics that light has no mass—it has energy, but no mass. Doesn't weigh a damn thing, and yet, from its vantage, time doesn't even exist. At the speed of light, everything is everywhere all at once. Can you imagine that?"

"I don't like to think about those things."

"Why not? If you're so burdened by the weight of the truth, take a look up and see that it's all just an illusion. There's nothing really there."

"I don't think Jesus would say that."

Reverend Olson laughed. "All those gospels we wrote down to interpret what Jesus said and didn't say—those words have a lot of weight. Sometimes I think it might be easier to just doubt things.

Doubt everything. Just throw it all away and move to some shack in Michigan. You're from Michigan, right? You and Alphonse?"

Meredith nodded, quietly sliding away from the reverend. "When I think of it—of life back in Michigan—there was no clutter anywhere. No cooking gadgets or expensive dinnerware. No fear of collapse. No *to have and have not*. Just an airy cabin full of love and thoughts."

"So what about Alphonse and Rachel? Are they just . . . *clutter*?"

"Of course not," Meredith barked, just loud enough to catch herself. She could hear the traffic on Route 78, humming like the wind. The church custodian appeared in the chancel, sweeping dust into a stand-up bin. "Sometimes I want to go back there," Meredith said.

"To Michigan?"

She shook her head. "To the green room. I was so scared. I had to pee so bad, my back was killing me, and I thought I was dead. But I've never felt closer to Him. I could almost smell Him."

"What did He smell like?" The reverend looked frightened, and it occurred to Meredith that his line of questioning, curt and without testimony, might stem from his own angst, that perhaps he, like so many others of late, had been shaken.

"He smelled like fruit. Or Lysol. I can't tell the difference, but now I feel the urge to clean house, just throw out everything and start again."

"So why don't you?"

ALPHONSE PRIZED TUESDAYS BECAUSE it was his day off and he had the whole house to drink beer and eat pork. He would wake up late, cook a breakfast of bacon and eggs, which Meredith abhorred for its salt and cholesterol and all the wrong fats. He'd crack open his first beer after breakfast, head out to the deck, and turn on the radio to listen to some jackal lament the poisoning of America. He didn't care for the content so much as the company.

Since he'd demolished the deck to build a new one, his routine moved indoors. He didn't mind. He'd already had one benign tumor removed from his cheek, and a lifetime dose of sunlight only threatened more. Inside was good. Inside was safe. Here, among his things—the dartboard cabinet he never hung up, the rows of dead and half-dead succulents Meredith never watered, the empty printer box no one thought to throw out, and the shelves of Dean Koontz novels no one ever read—he could be still. It was clutter, he knew that, but it was also evidence of the life they had, the memories of a family. Here, with only his own thoughts to entertain him, Alphonse could fill in the gaps as he pleased.

The snap of the screen door stirred him from a catnap. He heard someone rummaging around the den, tearing open boxes and rattling dinnerware. Alphonse grabbed an empty bottle of Old Grand-Dad and tip-toed toward the racket, unfurling visions of heroism that would surely vanquish this recent plague of ufologists and church ladies. Any news is good news, as they say in public relations. That's all this was, this nonsense about UFOs and abductions—a PR problem.

Alphonse turned the corner to find his wife emptying the glass cupboard and stuffing her plates and bowls into a cardboard box. "What the hell are you doing? Why aren't you at work?"

Meredith hardly stole a glance at Alphonse as she grabbed a Sharpie and wrote *Mikasa* on the box. "We're gonna have a yard sale," she said.

"On a Tuesday? Are you crazy? Why aren't you at work?"

"Not today. Saturday. Gotta prepare early. Lotta rusty, moth-eaten filth in this den. Time to clean the temple."

LATER THAT DAY, ALPHONSE found Rachel in her room snapping Barbie dolls over her knee. He told her it's a yard sale, not a dump run, but Rachel shrugged and kept on snapping and Alphonse returned to his box marked *Misc #7*. At the very least, he thought, this junk could earn enough cash for groceries. The fact of Meredith's layoff kept needling its way into his thoughts, stirring dread he hadn't felt since the move west. He had overreacted to the news; he didn't need her to remind him. As soon as he'd tossed his beer at the wall and seen the foam drip down the peeling wallpaper, he knew he'd gone overboard. But Meredith kept calm and apologized and said what's done is done. So what else could he do but clean up his mess and go along with her ploy to empty the castle? He would apologize, too. In time. He promised himself that much. But first he needed to be alone.

After stuffing the seventh *Misc* box, Alphonse grabbed a Sharpie and some paper and got into the Windstar and drove to church. There, he posted a flyer advertising a yard sale at the home of Meredith and Alphonse Sanger. It would end up being his biggest mistake of the day.

THE SECOND TIME MEREDITH Sanger was abducted there were no spaceships or extraterrestrial beings or jazz-themed interrogations. This one was of a darker sort, an inward journey that began with a hasty pulse. At first they trickled in: the church hens and reporters and upstart bloggers eyeing a big break off the back of some blue-collar head case. None of them were interested in Meredith's Mikasa dinnerware set or Rachel's broken Barbie dolls or Alphonse's splintery dart cabinet. They wanted the story, which no longer had anything to do with God or aliens or visions of the divine, but Meredith herself.

What did God look like?

"All plastic cups are a dollar."

What do you think of the name Meredith the Martian?

"These are springs from a trampoline. We sold it after it catapulted me into the sage thicket."

Judith arrived with Cynthia and set off with questions about the donations that had been tendered under what they perceived to be fraudulent circumstances.

Everyone thought you were dead.

"We have a large VHS collection. Have you seen *Balto*?"

Cynthia combed through Rachel's box of Barbies, dangling snapped limbs like they were inedible lunchmeat.

Are they all broken?

"Twelve dollars for the Coors sign."

A boy with an adolescent mustache was fiddling with a microphone.

Give you fifty bucks if you tell us how you did it.

"Those EpiPens might be expired."

Rachel asked Cynthia if she wanted to see the rest of her collection. Cynthia laughed and said she didn't play with Barbies anymore. *Are you serious?* Alphonse was at the end of the driveway directing traffic, shouting something about this being a yard sale, not a sideshow.

How would you respond to critics who say you're lying about your abduction to get a book deal?

"This is a special edition Clue. It's missing Colonel Mustard."

Are you a liar, Meredith?

A Channel 4 news van came over the hill. Alphonse rushed over, waving his arms and pleading with the driver to turn around, but the van drove around him and parked on the street in front of the house. Within seconds a news crew was marching toward Meredith, led by a blonde reporter in a clay-colored coat. Meredith thought about running inside but didn't want to look like a coward in front of Rachel, who was busy defending the existence of her doll collection. Judith eyed the approaching news crew and said something about Meredith being the story of the week.

"Please," Meredith said, grabbing Judith's arm. She could feel her heart thumping in the veins of her arms. "I can't do this—not today. Will you—"

"What? Can't take the limelight, Meredith? Then maybe you shouldn't have stepped out onto the stage."

Alphonse was trying to box out the news crew, but they could see Meredith from across the lawn. The lens on the camera looked blacker than the eyes of a chuckwalla. Rachel tugged on her mother's arm and said let's go inside. A stranger said I can't believe our timing. Cynthia said I can't believe you still play with Barbies.

Then something grabbed Meredith, pulled her inward to a place where everyone she knew was a knickknack in a display case. They wore rictus grins and long fingernails. They pantomimed her abduction, holding Meredith down to witness a stage play of anxieties: chronic pain, the cost of braces, an unfinished deck, unemployment, the mockery of everyone she'd thought was a friend. A distant husband. A faithless daughter. Her heart was racing, thumping in the dark and reminding her of the voice in the garden. It was so fast. She wanted to dial it back like the hands of a clock—dial that, too, back to the evening in the desert. If she could do it all again, she would insist on interrogating them—not the other way around. This was *her* stage, you see, not theirs. This was *her* home. And if they wanted to know when Miles Davis is, then they need to answer some questions first.

Okay, someone said.

Okay, what?

Tell us what you want to know.

Ah, well. I have to think about it.

We've got all the time in the world.

All the time?

Well, most of it. You? Not so much. You're on the plane of time.

Am I dying?

Yes, but not in the way you think. You're always dying. All you people are always dying. It's fascinating.

But Rachel—I need to see her—

Let us explain. You're not dying in what you would call now.

I'm not? Then what's happening to me?

You're alright. You just need a break. Someone to talk to. Maybe a better diet.

I've got my family.

But you don't talk to them.

They're so distant. It's like I don't even know them.

These things move around—or, I guess you would say, change. *We can see how they change around you, how they warp and buckle between birth and death. The duality of it. It's fascinating. We wish you could see it, what you call "the future." But you can't. It's fascinating.*

What's my future?

Something over there. Something you can't change. Like a wave before it crashes.

So what do I do?

Ride the crest while you can. Be the puny little point of light that you are. Be beautiful. Be the thing we love about you. It's so easy. It's so easy to just be what you're meant to be.

It is?

Well, for us it is. Go back and try it out.

FOR A SECOND MEREDITH thought she had had a heart attack. Staring up at the swarm of reporters and busybodies, circling like buzzards, she had a vision within a vision—that of a motherless Rachel and a widowed Alphonse whose idle Tuesdays indulged every excess. She knew their marriage was not what it used to be, but there, in that moment, she saw the entirety of it stretched out like a roll of film— each frame home to a different memory or dream or cloudy augury. It was not all laughter and ice cream cones. There was ugliness and death, too. But at least it was shared. She was grateful to have seen it, if only in a moment, because it spoke to some dormant spirit, a long-lost fragment that had no trouble hurling invective at strangers while Channel 4 News was watching, no doubt providing the perfect B-roll for some venomous bumper about *Mad Meredith the Martian Matriarch.* Let them have it. Let them inject their venom and slither off into the night.

But she had only fainted. She should have recognized the signs of a panic attack, of which Meredith was no stranger. The fainting, though, that was something new—something to see Dr. Ramirez about. But then there's the deductible, which surely they'd have to declare bankruptcy to reach. They say a healthy diet and exercise keeps the deductible away. Maybe there's wisdom in that.

For the rest of the day Alphonse doted on his wife, bringing her glass after glass of water and refusing any wish for Pepsi or peanut butter cookies. He would make a dinner of fried asparagus and fish sticks. Rachel hated it. So did Meredith, and so did Alphonse, for that matter. But it was a start.

A knock on the front door interrupted the meal. Meredith answered it. Detective Árbenz looked tired and more irritated than usual. "What's this I hear about a family of worker bees stinging folks who came looking for tchotchkes?"

"Bunch of dirty vultures!" Rachel shouted from the dinner table. "They were swarming us—"

"Quiet, Rachel," Meredith said, turning back to the detective. "We only wanted to have a yard sale."

"We were decluttering the house," Alphonse shouted, also from the table. "And this gaggle of snoopers and muckrakers flew in and started suffocating us, suffocating my wife with all their stupid questions. She's been through a lot, you know."

"Decluttering is one thing," Árbenz said. "Littering in the same swoop as aggravated assault is almost impressive. And doubly illegal. I received a call from a Judith Peterson that y'all hurled dinner plates and Barbie dolls at her and her daughter as they fled the scene."

"Like we said," Rachel shouted. "Bunch of dirty vultures!"

"Look," Árbenz said, "I'm a detective with the Kern County Sheriff's Office. I got real crimes to investigate. This morning a dude huffed up on gasoline and bath salts climbed a firehouse in Buttonwillow and started shouting about the end times. I can't be following up on this sideshow about Meredith the Martian. It's gossip. You hear me?"

"Of course," Meredith said.

"Ten four," Alphonse shouted.

"Alright then," Árbenz said, turning to leave. "And please clean up your lawn. There's too much—"

She froze in the doorway. A stillness fell around the detective as her eye caught something outside, something out of shot from Meredith. Whatever it was had washed the front lawn in milky white light.

"Detective?" Meredith approached Árbenz. She looked for some sign of life but found only stillness. She looked out into the night and heard perfect silence. The wind had died. A car had stopped in the middle of the road. A plane overhead was frozen in midair. All was still save for the milky white light, which blanketed the yard, gelling like a lava lamp and illuminating the mounds of dusty cookbooks and VHS tapes and broken pepper shakers she'd yet to clean up.

Meredith turned to find her husband and daughter also motionless, still sitting at the kitchen table and glowing beneath the lamp like subjects in chiaroscuro. They were smiling at her, as if she had just made a joke—and not a dumb joke, but something clever and age-appropriate. Confused, yet oddly at ease, Meredith remembered the time they drove across country. Rachel was hardly a toddler, and all they owned was what they could fit in the Windstar. They'd gotten lost more than once, even ran out of gas the night Alphonse opted to have one too many beers at Applebee's. Meredith had to hike two miles down the road to collect a fresh tank. When she returned she found Rachel sleeping in Alphonse's arms in the back seat of the Windstar, the interior light haloed overhead. She would later describe the tableau to Alphonse, recalling how the all-night journey had been worth it for that one image, frozen in time. He said that sounds nice, then twisted the antenna and smacked the TV for better reception.

Now Meredith recalled the memory for the first time in years, and once again she was alone. All was still. All was silent. If she could stretch this moment out to eternity, to set so many eyes upon her endless nativity, she would happily do it, suffering the passions to stand as a witness to the family who needed her, even as the sound of a distant, lonely trumpet echoed overhead.

Breaking the Seal

Marianne Leone

Dear Father Generic Irish Name:

(I can't remember your name or face, just your collar and ankle-length man dress.)

I'm not good at keeping secrets, father. Right now as a side note, I want to assure any friends that somehow happen to read this—for other people's secrets I have extreme, Sicilian-level *omerta*. But for my own? Not so much. I'm a blabbermouth by nature and an actress by trade so I don't have many good secrets left at this point because they've all been blabbed.

But I feel like it is time to break the seal of the confessional.

When they told us at the retreat that due to the new rules of the church, confession was now going to be a face-to-face deal—I'll admit it threw me, the face-to-face thing. I was seventeen years old and about to graduate from the parochial school I had gone to since kindergarten. All the girls in my class had spent a weekend at the Holy Family Retreat House where we were supposed to be praying and getting ready for our roles as Catholic wives and mothers in the outside world after high school. It was the late sixties. There were no other options at the time, except nurse or teacher or secretary. The night before the face to face, you and some of the other priests had—inexplicably and creepily—screened Fellini's *La Strada* for us, a film with Giulietta Masina and Anthony Quinn. Anthony Quinn is a strong man in a circus who buys Giulietta Masina from her impoverished mother. He is brutal to Giulietta Masina, and he abandons her in the end, but this drives him crazy. Nobody got why we were seeing this film, but I got that I wanted to do what Giulietta Masina was doing—shine like I was lit from within and make people laugh and cry. I made her my patron saint of acting, so thank you for that. Now I knew what I wanted to do after high school.

The face-to-face confession was supposed to be the last holy ritual we did before we were able to go home. It was a required thing, like when you go before a parole board.

At the time, I finally had a boyfriend who wasn't monosyllabic and who read books and could quote Oscar Wilde and Edward Gorey at will, which made me love him. We were romantically dry humping in rooms heaped with coats at teenage parties and I was writing profane poetry for him about chalices of flesh, inspired by Rimbaud and Baudelaire and Sylvia Plath. For this required confession I had kind of been counting on the usual setup that even non-Catholics have seen in films or read about—the little booth, the blackout curtain, the darkness, and the further anonymity of the face-level grate that distorts your features so that you're unrecognizable afterwards in a crowd of other girls. Instead, you opened the door to a prissy living room with two pale satin-upholstered chairs facing each other. I was awkward and confused and the lace mantilla I was wearing got caught in my mouth and made me choke. You looked eager and smiley. Was I supposed to kneel before you while you sat? No, you informed me, I could sit in my chair facing you while I said the ritual words: "bless me father, for I have sinned."

I realize that when I told you about the boy touching me it was partly because of my impulse control issue and partly due to my being an incorrigible show-off. I kind of wanted to brag about my new boyfriend who wasn't even Catholic and had a grandfather who was Chinese and wore his glossy black hair long and had an upper lip that mesmerized me because it curved into a natural sneer. You weren't impressed, as I recall. You got right down to business and asked if I let the boy touch me and I said that I did (I was absurdly proud of this. Most boys just told me "you're weird" and walked away at Catholic Youth Organization dances). You got very serious and killjoy and told me that you couldn't grant me absolution unless I promised to never do it again. And the way you said that! That you, as the agent and direct representative and mouthpiece of God would deny me forgiveness, and the idea that I would remain forever tainted by sin, unforgiven, with a compromised, blackened soul—that terrified me. For about a minute.

And then, for the first time in a long time, I listened to my mother, even though my mother and I were mortal enemies at the time. Do you know what a *mangiapreti* is, father? The literal translation is "priest eater" in Italian. It also means anticleric. My mother was from Italy and she was a *mangiapreti* even though she sent me to Catholic school. She thought it had to be better because you paid for it. It wasn't. It really wasn't. I remembered when I was a little kid and cried because she never went to confession and I was afraid she would burn in hell and not go to heaven where I planned to reside for all eternity. She was rolling out the Sunday macaroni at the time and she cut off two strands and twisted them together. She showed them to me and said they were called *strozzapreti*—priest stranglers. Because when she was in Italy and they didn't have much to eat, the priest would invite himself over for dinner and he would eat a big plate of *strozzapreti* that was supposed to be for the whole family and they would end up going hungry and he should choke on it and that's why they're called priest stranglers. I told her that you were the human representative of God on earth and strangling a priest was murder, but then she said that the priest making them *morta di fame* was also murder, just slower. She said to be careful around priests and never to let them touch me. I thought she was crazy and prayed for her and hoped her craziness would spare her from the eternal fire.

Turns out, she was smart, my mother.

So, you may be wondering why I talked about breaking the seal of the confessional at the beginning of this letter, when you're the one bound to secrecy. Well, father, I wanted to thank you: that confession was the beginning of a transfer of power. I took the power from you to stand in for God as her representative. And that's why it's me breaking the bonds of the confessional and not you, so no worries on your part.

On that day, I told you that I would never do it again. Only I didn't specify that I would never let the boy touch me again. I just agreed that I would never do it again.

And I didn't even really know at the time that when I said I would never do it again that it would mean that I would never again, in the dark or face to face in full daylight, confess my sins to a man who claimed to be standing in for God.

Sincerely,

Christina the Astonishing Falcone

Softly

Mary Pauer

WE REACH FOR THE PACKAGE OF PORKCHOPS AT THE SAME TIME. OUR FINGERS do not touch, but stick to the plastic wrap that surrounds those lovely cuts. The film molds to my fingertips. I see the curly hair on the back of his hand.

The last two chops. Maybe the last pieces of meat in the entire store, in the entire universe. Well, meat might still be on the hoof somewhere, but these are pink and round and thick on the bone, ready for my indoor grill.

I do grill veggies in a pan designed for sliced, slippery peppers, onions, mushrooms, zucchini. Sometimes I lay half-mooned shrimp in that pan, letting the heat pass through, turning the gray-gray crustaceans to a Shirley Temple pink, ready for me to pop in my mouth and suck the tenderness away.

But these chops are to be thrown directly on the sizzling metal rack, to be flipped only once. They will be cross-hatched, crackling crisp fat caressing the charred flesh.

In the aisle, I feel myself grow faint with hunger, my stomach rumbles in anticipation; then I see his hand curl around my package. I don't look up. I won't remove my hand and cede to him. I growl, throaty like a GTO muscle car idling at stoplight, like the sound my not-quite feral cat utters with a mouse in his jaws.

The man says, almost in a whisper. "I'm sorry. Please, take them."

Through my side glance I see him fade down aisle three, the one with canned fruits.

I think about him, his fear. If this were the last pack of porkchops, ever, would I have clamped my teeth to his neck? At home, would I grill both chops, and luxuriate until my stomach revolted? Or, would I take a small bite each day, distilling the taste, teasing myself until the end?

Slowly, so as not to draw attention to my prize, I slip them into my cart, nonchalantly, push along the now empty shelf, turn into the dairy aisle, cooling the heat of my desire among the yoghurts, cottage cheeses, and whipped creams. I imagine depressing the nozzle into my open mouth, billowing mounds of airy sweetness from the canister dribbling along my jawline before I swallow.

Nightflight to Venus

Sarah Kontopoulos

WHAT WOULD IT TAKE TO GO EVEN FARTHER NEXT TIME? TO BE AWAY LONGER? Judith's eyes traced the border of the pale-yellow water stain on the white acoustic ceiling tile hanging above her bed. It seeped across the metal tile grid into the next tile, blooming into a pallid rust flower.

If I start here in Seattle at ten o'clock, where could I go in four hours? Or six? She weighed and measured places and their distance from her body.

Last night it had taken just over an hour to travel with her mind to the MoClips cabin on the Washington Peninsula and back—or so said her standard issue wall clock. About half the time it took her physical body to get there by car.

She was surprised at first, to project out of her sleeping body. Disbelieving, she'd hovered over it up by the rust flower watching her own peaceable breathing for several minutes. How many years had it been since she had separated this way? She couldn't remember. And when did I get so shrunken and old? Also, unclear.

And then, in a blink, Judith stood in MoClips on the dark rocky shore. Black water lapped cold at her toes. Its nighttime chill was muted, but she felt it. I guess you never forget how. Like riding a bike.

A group of surprised mallards glided by quacking their rebuke: "What are you doing here so late? My word, and in her nightdress no less!"

Busybodies.

Judith looked up the slope past the beach grass to the vacant dusky cabin. She and Steven had bought it in the late '60s, over fifty years before. He'd been gone ten years, and she missed his calm strength every day. His even keel–ness.

Ordinarily, her family would be curled up inside the house. In the early evening, the cloud tinted front sheers drawn open, a cozy television and table lamp glow illuminating the living room. They watched movies and cuddled together under snug blankets Judith knit for them. Later, upstairs, children and grandchildren drifted in a sweet deep slumber, a single night owl nosing a book.

I did get back early this time.

Back in her room and in her bed, Judith heard a car crunch over gravel in the parking lot outside. Its headlights reflected off the closed vinyl window blinds, casting shuttering searchlight lines into the room. They hurriedly ticked across the minty curtain next to her, as if from a distorted rectangular disco ball, and then across the coordinating wall at the foot of her bed, before disappearing. Afterward, the room lay still except for the nocturnal whirring of her roommate's CPAP machine.

How far could she go if she left early? Maybe Sedona.

Further? The desert . . . Yes, back there.

But in one night?

Not this night, though they wouldn't be woken for at least two more hours. Judith centered her hands across her belly over the fine sheet and thin coverlet draped over her. Both also in mint. Despite their bareness, they cocooned her.

Next time.

She closed her eyes and slept.

THE NEXT NIGHT SHE fell asleep earlier but didn't make it to lucid until halfway through the night. Too late to go farther.

So instead, she went back to her parents' home on Whidbey Island and dangled her legs off the southern edge of the asphalt roof, overlooking the vegetable garden. In the darkness, loose shingle grit scratched the back of her knees and quadriceps as she swung her legs, sprinkling crushed stone granules down below.

Her parents had favored root vegetables: orange Tendersweet carrots, buttery gold potatoes, Walla Walla sweet onions, and ivory sugar beets.

Tell it again, the kid would beg. So, Dad told again the Montana harvest tales of running behind the rickety beet wagon tottering on its wooden wheels, brothers and sisters competing to see who could mine the most "white gold." And how he'd learned at dusk from the farm hands all he knew, and ever needed to, about playing baseball.

Well, it used to grow vegetables, anyway.

Now, large concrete pavers mapped out a different garden, for repose. It grew resin wicker furniture, a shade umbrella closed in nyctinasty, an ashy fire pit, and sprouted a hot tub instead of beets. The new family living there were all asleep, like her. Do any of them wander too?

Next door she peered through the top row of windows of the smaller of two Tuscan-style villas. Her breath left a barely noticeable residue of fog on the glass.

Even the fusion red Tesla Roadster inside slumbered, dreaming of long Sunday drives to Oak Harbor. It was likely unaware that its garage succeeded the farm outbuilding of her birth by seventy years, and her birth preceded Whidbey Island's first hospital by almost forty.

The twilight morning sky overhead had started lightening toward dawn, so she blinked herself back.

"GOOD MORNING, MISS EVELYN. Good morning, Miss Judith." From above she saw Marisol squish across their viridescent room in her white Angel Lites to open the vinyl blinds to the morning light.

Marisol rubbed Judith's shoulder. "Time to wake up, Missus. It's a very beautiful morning." She walked past the dividing curtain to Judith's roommate Evelyn's side. Evelyn's alert and anxious face lay in wait.

"Marisol, I had the most disturbing dream last night." Evelyn held her right arm out expectantly.

"Oh, reeaally? Tell me, Miss Evelyn." Marisol reached back, grasping the arm, both women leveraging their angle to raise Evelyn to a seated position so she could turn and face her nighttime guardian, a gray bedside commode. Marisol lifted her hands to its foam-gripped armrests.

I wonder if Marisol knows her hair is thinning on top. I'll bet she can't see it. Judith would never tell her.

"I was at the Friends Meeting House, waiting for the Spirit to find me. It hadn't found anybody else yet either. Suddenly, I felt it! I stood up! I was going to speak, and then . . . and then . . ."

Evelyn's eyes widened, whites bared, as spasmodic rigidity tightened in her neck and shoulders, "when I stood up, I was the only one with clothes on!"

"Oh no, Miss Evelyn. That is very upsetting. Don't be embarrassed. It was just a dream." Marisol winked and patted her back. Evelyn's body released.

Evelyn was a Quaker, a nudist Quaker, who frequently disrobed. That had been her comfortable normal for a lifetime, why would she change now? Two or three times a week visitors passing their room viewed her splayed, naked on her bed, which was the first inside their room. Lately, forgetting where she was, Evelyn had started undressing in the dining room, or the rehab gym. The staff were unfazed, and kindly directed her to her room.

Marisol helped Evelyn settle onto the commode seat and called to Judith over the light dribbling sounds of urine tapping into the hollow bucket underneath it, "Alright, Miss Judith, almost your turn. Time to wake up, Sleeping Beauty!" She chuckled.

Marisol pulled back the curtain and stood over Judith.

"Are you awake, Missus?!"

Judith cracked her eyes open. "Good morning, Miss Marisol," she said.

* * *

IT WAS JUST BEFORE midnight on Friday when Judith was startled awake.

"Oh! I'm wet! Help! I'm weeet! Mamaaa!"

They put Evelyn in generous adult briefs, that slipped on like underwear. But two or three nights a week when a brief failed to contain her, a slow-creeping, sour ammonia spill overflowed to the bed pad below, soaking the bedsheets, and wafted over to Judith's side.

Judith prayed as she pulled the call light string. Please, please, let it be Tony. Minutes passed.

"I'm all wet. I-I need to get up. I have to go potty!"

From the other side of the curtain, she heard Evelyn struggle to sit up and then flop back. Thank God. The alternative was disaster if she ever succeeded. She had fallen before.

After fifteen minutes Judith knew it was him. The fastest he'd come was half an hour. The slowest—two hours?

And then he'd yelled at Evelyn, "Ugh, again? What are you, a baby? I should rub your nose in it. That would teach you."

Why does he repeat that garbage? Doesn't he hear his father's voice? Judith would never tell him. And she wished once more that they didn't need him.

After almost an hour, Evelyn had reached her limit.

"Riiiiick! I'm weeeeet," she screamed.

Even within her perpetually shifting fog, Evelyn eventually remembered who was in charge, who could help her—if he would—when she sat in her own stink and wet.

Rick loped into the room then, first to Judith's side to reset the call light, and then to Evelyn's.

"Rick! I'm all wet!"

Silence. Judith heard another CNA enter the room.

Judith pictured Evelyn imploring them with the whites of her eyes, while the two men ignored her. Wordlessly they transferred her to the commode, stripped her clothing and sheets, remade the bed, redressed Evelyn, and put her back to bed. The sound of one pair of feet leaving the room. Then a quick, dull papery thump against something on the bed.

"Owww!" Evelyn howled. "I didn't mean to do it! Ri-hi-hi-hick!" she began to wail.

Judith imagined he'd shoved her shoulder or her bad knee. Not hard, not enough to really hurt, but enough to startle, intimidate, and upset. Judith's stomach burned.

LATE ON SATURDAY NIGHT, though by then it was early Sunday, Judith returned from another journey away from her sleeping self. She delayed going back to her body and bed, and wandered the quiet halls, pausing at the nurses' station.

Rick sat staring at his cell phone, while another man fiddled with the brown plastic stir stick in a white Styrofoam cup of vending machine coffee. Like Rick, the long blue lanyard around his neck was printed all over with the same repeating acronym: CNA—certified nursing assistant. But the nametag attached to it was flipped over, and Judith couldn't remember his name.

"How's your kid, man?" the CNA asked.

Rick was engrossed in a video on his phone and didn't hear.

". . . codenamed the Stargate Project. This secret US military unit was co-created by the Defense Intelligence Agency, or 'DIA,' and Stanford University's remote viewing lab, called 'SRI,' and was active from the early '70s until 1995 when it was closed due to lack of replicable findings. Reportedly, only ten men remained as remote viewers at the time . . ."

Judith rolled her eyes. Ten men, ten men. They never got it right. Not ten "men" who were remote viewers, ten couples.

You're right, but you know we can't tell anyone, Steven would say.

One paper misreported it twenty-five years ago, and now the story perpetuated on and on in every new iteration.

You know it's classified information. Steven gently reminding her again. Let it go, Jude. And she had, mostly.

"Yo, Rick. How's Shelley?" Rick looked up at his daughter's name.

"She's good. Yeah, thanks for askin'. She's real good. I hadda fight her mom to see her but I got every third weekend."

"That's great. So, you get a weekend off every three weeks now, huh?" The CNA chortled. Judith leisurely floated down the hallway away from them, only half listening to the conversation.

"Yeah, really. Tell you I broke my old record? Zero days off in fifteen months before my first weekend with Shell. The D-O-N at Majestic Pines was pissed. They never have enough CNAs and that first weekend they had a state visit. You know how management likes extra padding when State's in the building."

"Riiiight," she heard the other man say. Judith turned the corner and entered her room.

The next weekend after a breezy trip around the Seattle Great Wheel, Judith looked down at the scene unfolding on Evelyn's side of the curtain. Rick hulked over a sleeping Evelyn with his right arm pulled back. Quickly, with his pointer and middle fingers he jabbed Evelyn's hip hard, followed by her neck. She cried out in her sleep.

The nights Rick worked, Evelyn woke crying more than usual, and now Judith understood why. When he wound up again Judith swooped down and finger punched his shoulder, throwing him off balance.

"Enough," she hissed.

Rick gasped and recoiled, hearing nothing. Just be satisfied with scaring him, she told herself. But the slow sear had reawakened in her stomach.

Rick hurriedly searched the room and bathroom, checking and rechecking that the women were asleep in their beds, and then, rubbing his shoulder, hurried toward the doorway. Judith held up the hem of her nightdress to kick him in the backside, propelling him through the door.

Yelping, Rick ran up the hallway, checking over his shoulder for the poltergeist or serial killer that would surely follow. Judith flew behind and alongside him in an invisible rage. The scorch in her belly fueled an inferno. Every few seconds she assaulted some part of him—elbowed his ear or struck the back of his knees making him pitch forward.

How do you like me now? She seethed.

"Gotta take a leak," Rick called to the other CNA as he rushed by him.

Judith launched herself into the bathroom ahead of him, so when Rick locked the door she was already inside. He hugged himself, shaking and muttering.

"Don't— don't hurt me, please, don't hurt me," he whimpered.

Judith moved in close, so they were nearly nose to nose, examining his face. He was younger than she'd thought, with a lingering eruption of facial acne. Not a day over twenty-five, she guessed. He was just a kid really. A boy-man. He stared through her, waiting.

What's your best-case scenario here, Jude? Steven's rational voice cut in with a favorite crisis question from their CIA days. She circled Rick and studied him in the mirror from behind.

When Rick looked into the mirror he shrieked. They were faint, but Judith's outline and face were visible behind him.

They can see us in mirrors?! Judith felt the incredulous thrill of an unexpected new power.

Rick looked around cautiously, bracing for what might come. Ghost in the mirror, yes; ghost behind him, no.

Before Judith could make her next move, he spoke to her:

"Mom? Is . . . is it you?"

Hmm, didn't see that coming. Well, whatever worked. Judith gave a dramatic nod.

"I thought it was you. I miss you so much, Mom . . . Ashley left, and-and Shelley's eight now . . . but, you probably know all that." He paused.

"I'm tired, Mama," he whispered. A tear streaked down Rick's face and fizzled out Judith's anger. Even so, she scowled and cuffed the back of his head. He still needed to get the message.

"Why are you so angry? I never hit Ty again after you died, I swear," he offered. Closer, getting closer. Judith prodded him in the hip and neck where he had poked Evelyn.

"Ouch! The old lady? Is that why you're mad? Shit. She's crazy! And she makes so much work." With both hands Judith shoved him hard in the shoulders causing him to lurch toward the sink. "Okay, okay, I get it, I'll leave her alone."

Finally.

Satisfied, Judith backed up, preparing to blink back to her room.

"Wait! Don't go! Don't leave me, again. Please!"

His vulnerability surprised her, and he appeared in that moment to be about twelve, all knock-knees and horse teeth. Too big for his skinny boy-man face, and far too young to know about divorce or working so many long hours and days without rest. In his face she saw that there was still a choice about the kind of man he would become. Steven's question bobbed in her head.

And then, surprising herself this time, Judith stepped forward and slowly put her arms around him, embracing him deeply. The hug was brief, but it felt real, as real can be. She wished for him to be the kind of man he might be, and hoped it was still possible, before blinking out.

Judith kept tabs on Rick through the summer and early fall. Made sure he didn't see her, of course. He wasn't friendly, but he never hurt or yelled at Evelyn again, or anyone else that she could see.

LATE ON THE LAST night, near the end of October, Judith lies awake in the darkened room listening to the velvet purring coming from Evelyn's side of the room.

Overhead, the rust flower has been replaced with two new white ceiling tiles. Suspended over her, they portend an inviting fresh start. In the hallway, she hears Marisol squelch by, and, after smoothing the coverlet over her body, Judith falls asleep content.

Nineteen hours later, Judith stands barefoot in her nightgown facing westward at Sotol Vista Overlook, in the Chihuahuan desert. The light abates toward dusk and a black-tailed jack rabbit leaps through her legs. The warm air smells fresh and dry.

It took more than half the time it would to drive here. Three hours slower than when she came regularly in the 1970s—the same decade as the building of Whidbey Island hospital.

Not bad for an old lady.

The sun set more than an hour ago and she's missed the dramatic chiaroscuro play of bright sunset and shadows across the desert plant life: rosetophilous scrub, feather dalea, agave lechuguilla, and others. Now the same flora bear witness as the sky around them moves from the sunset auburns and golds of civilian twilight to the darkened indigo of nautical twilight, where only dark shapes appear silhouetted against the dimming background of the sky. The deep canyon awaits in the distance.

SHE IMAGINES HOW IT went early that morning when Marisol tried to wake her—

"Yes, Miss Evelyn, I'm coming!" Marisol on Evelyn's side turning off her CPAP. Pulling back the covers to help Evelyn sit up. Evelyn puffing to catch her breath. Then whisking back the curtain to Judith's side.

"Are you awake, Missus? Time to wake up, Sleeping Beauty."

No response from Judith, save slow shallow breaths and a Mona Lisa smile.

And then the LPN, and then the RN, and then the nursing director trying all they can to wake her up.

—Now she glides through the cool night air toward Santa Elena Canyon where the Rio Grande emerges between the V-shaped canyon's sharp vertical limestone cliffs. Half the canyon lies on the southern,

Mexican Sierra Ponce side, and half on the northern, US Mesa de Anguila side. It means the river has two names: Rio Grande and Rio Bravo.

Does the canyon know it's a dual citizen? Why would it care about such a fleeting temporal designation? It hardly stirs at her arrival anyway. She isn't the first one here. Long before, the Spanish and Comanches came, and before them the Apaches, the Jumanos, the Chisos, and more before them. This place knows them all—

They had to call the doctor to try and wake her. It took him several hours to come. She was just sleeping after all.

—Above her the night sky is cloudless, and hanging over her head now, against the onyx violet expansiveness of space, is the dazzling, tilted, silver and white banner of the Milky Way. Under it, nearer the horizon, Venus's bright glimmer—always chasing the sun at this time of year. Perhaps Steven went to Venus. Perhaps he's waiting there now. And she wonders again . . . what would it take to go even farther? To be away longer? She's not hungry or cold, or tired. Maybe she never has to return, to go there—

Though she's breathing and has the smile, the doctor cannot wake her either. So, she'll sleep peacefully for several days and slip away a few later. That sounds just right.

—And then, thinking it over one last time, Judith blinks, and is gone.

Anthropologist

Bergita Bugarija

I SHIMMIED LOOSE MY WEDDING RING. IT HAD TO COME OFF SO I COULD PLAY *cajón*, the drum I'd been messing around with for a few weeks. Last year, after I'd left full-time work, I put together a world music band with some neighbors to feel less suburban, less mom, less stuck. I sang until I saw Raiz, the percussionist, straddle a boxy drum and spank its front panel, and I wanted to give it a try. My jewelry clanked and scraped against the wood, so for practices I took my wedding band off along with my bracelets and hadn't thought twice about it. But tonight I would be ringless in public.

Was I ready to drum my bare fingers away at Corrida tapas bar? At first the whole thing felt daring, then unhinged, then a little pathetic. I looked up at my reflection in the mirror. I'd done my makeup like I used to when I sang in a punk band in college. The smoky eyes that stared back at me made me feel like an impostor in my suburban master bath. I ran my hand under the faucet to help slide the ring off and covered the drain with a washcloth in case it dislodged too abruptly and slid down. I twisted and pulled but it wouldn't give, as if it was welded to me.

Then, a ping in my back pocket. I pushed the ring back down and pulled out my phone, tapping the email icon. The study on loyalty for Unity Mutual had landed in my inbox. Was I available?, they asked. Consulting gigs for the consumer anthropologists I used to work for had gotten sparse, so each one felt like a rush. That I was still getting commissions meant my thoughts, deep and brilliant, mattered. *Available*, I answered. Details would follow shortly, they replied.

I strutted down the steps of my colonial in dark jeans, a loosely fitted black satin top, and layered necklaces, their mismatched beads in textured black and an occasional pop of silver giving me an air of intrigue without tempting pity. There was nothing sadder than a middle-aged stay-at-home mom trying to be a rock star.

I found my husband, Dan, in the kitchen, crouched under the island with a paper towel scooping up the after-dinner crumbs. His hairy butt crack stuck out of his sweatpants.

"Kids?" Dan said from the floor.

"Homework," I said. "Hopefully."

"Could you imagine my dad, or yours, doing this?" He wiped the floor clean of flattened fried chicken pieces in one swipe. Chicken I'd made from scratch.

He did this—asked questions he wanted me to answer in a particular way: No, darling, I can't imagine. A husband helping his wife with the household grind? I'm so lucky to have you, my thrift store designer find.

As he stood he bumped his head on the island lip.

"Times change," I said, checking myself in the hallway mirror. I ran my fingers through my hair to mess it up. Couldn't risk killing my rock cred with a symmetrical bob before even setting my butt on the drum.

"They sure do." Dan came over and kissed me, a quick peck, his outstretched hand holding the dirty paper towel so it wouldn't touch my outfit. "That's a fun getup," he said as he headed toward the couch. Live music was not his thing. Watching an assembly line make locomotive parts? Pink hot dog goo being pushed into the casing? That was his thing. The mechanical repetition relaxed him, he said, after a grueling day of litigating.

Another email alert vibrated in my pocket. I skimmed through the Unity Mutual files. Business problem: customer retention crisis.

Demographic: suburban, skew male, white, six-figure household income, a couple of kids. The usual suckers eager to put their money in UM's oh-so-caring, greedy hands. I scrolled to the research objectives: reposition the brand from *more, more, more* to *loyalty*. We want to understand what loyalty means, the objectives implored. How it's built, how it's maintained, what makes it, what tests it, what destroys it.

Dan could give them an answer without a fancy anthropological study. Well, Unity Mutual, he'd say, deliver on your promise. Do what you're supposed to. Don't be a dick. Don't betray the trust.

I put the phone in my back pocket. "I'm off," I said. "Don't wait up."

Dan lifted his hand from where he'd burrowed under the couch throw, his attention under the spell of a bolt and screw production line.

CORRIDA TAPAS BAR ON a Monday night was a sad place.

"That's why you guys are here," said the owner, whose name was Joe. He handed us each a shot of mezcal. Nemo, Bond, and Raiz swigged; I got my lips wet. Two back-to-back bouts of human gestation followed by years of breastfeeding will do cruel things to one's alcohol tolerance. And I had to drive myself home.

Nemo and Bond hooked up the guitars.

Raiz sat the *cajón* behind my mic, tapped the soundboard. "Show 'em how it's done," he said, nodding to me.

Monday night at Corrida was the perfect setting for a middle-aged rookie to practice in public. The place was empty save for an old guy in flannel-lined Crocs at the bar taming rubbery octopus with a steak knife and the young couple in oversized sweatshirts and plump undereye bags at the back table, a baby asleep in the stroller parked next to them. The room was as quiet as a cafeteria at off hours. Every clank of the silverware from the kitchen, every squeak of a rag polishing glasses echoed, and the dim lighting garnished the ambiance with the charm of a survivalist pit.

"You need to take that off," Raiz said, his hands busy laying out his percussion toys. He tilted his chin toward my left hand, where I still held the shot glass.

"No worries, mezcal is not part of the costume," I said.

"Not that, the ring."

"Ah, yes."

I wiggled the band halfway up my finger, then slowed down as if inching on a diving board, debating was I about to take the plunge into the frigid unknown. Just when the ring was about to come off my hand, I pushed it back down to the root of the finger.

Loyalty. What tests it?

Overanalyzing was my favorite pastime. Before it claimed me as a victim, I took the ring off. It would be fine in my jacket's zippered pocket for a couple of hours. Time to put on the show, give the people of Brandywine Hill some world music.

I straddled the drum and smacked it across the front, like I knew what I was doing. The guy at the bar dropped his knife. That spank rang louder than I intended. No going back.

First, some Cuban folk, where I made my beats subtle and pulsing, Nemo and Bond spread the bolero groove like warm butter over the guitar strings, and Raiz rustled the maracas. Then an old-school *fandango*. My warmed-up hands traversed the soundboard, top to sides, while the guitars played an unruly melody and the castanets went wild. By *cante jondo* I slapped the *cajón*, as if unshackled. It boomed with deep timbre and my fingers melted with the riff. I sang with the drum's sparse beat supporting my voice and giving it color, spice, a dash of saffron in the paella. Sweat trickled down my sensible top. I whipped my hair left and right, my parting line erased.

When I opened my eyes, I saw the baby on the woman's lap clapping, parts of slobbered tortilla pasted to each hand.

"Well, that was different," Flannel Crocs said as he handed his credit card to the bartender.

"Percussion *and* singing after three rehearsals," Raiz said, shaking his head admiringly. "Anything you can't do?" He looked at me like he saw me for the first time, eyes wide and focused.

I blushed.

Nemo clapped.

Bond took off his guitar. "Ole!"

THE NEXT DAY, TUESDAY—grocery store and dry cleaner—started like any other: whiny.

"Mom, Dylan toasted my bagel on three."

"Dylan, next time can you please toast Lily's bagel on—what, Lily?"

"Three and a half."

"Three and a half. Okay?" I said, leaning on the kitchen island, face in my laptop screen.

"Fine," Dylan said. "What are you reading?"

"About this drum I played last night at Corrida," I said.

"I thought you just sang."

"Me too," I said.

Dan glanced at the article as he passed behind me, lox in hand.

"Looks like a box."

The kids chuckled.

"It *is* a box. It says here that African slaves in Peru unloaded the boxes off ships and then at the end of the day, when they could rest and have some fun, they'd sit on a box like on a saddle and beat the front board with their palms and fingers to make music."

Dan widened his eyes like he always did when pretending to care. Dylan yawned. Lily ate her bagel without using hands, a strand of her hair slathered with cream cheese. I took a loud breath.

"Then later this guy Paco de Lucía brought it to Spain. He was a famous flamenco guitarist and he really liked this drum and wanted to make it work with flamenco so he added the snares inside to make the beats vibrate."

"I bet an assembly line spits them out dozens per minute," Dan said.

I rolled my eyes, and he saw it.

"I mean, doesn't seem like there's much to it," he added.

Take it for a ride, I didn't say out loud.

THE SIGHT OF THE school building made me shudder at every drop-off: brick walls, tinted windows, an edifice as nondescript as the failed corporate headquarters of an abandoned mall. What could anyone possibly learn in that soulless box aside from conformism? Good time as any to practice gratitude for my band, my voice, my drum. The carpool caravan spat out parents and kids under the awning. I blew Lily and Dylan a kiss and turned to get back in the car.

"You look nice."

I turned around. Mr. Irvin, Lily's teacher, smiled. I looked left and right; he must have meant the compliment for someone else. I wore my regular workweek uniform: gray shirt, dark jeans, black cardigan, hair in a messy ponytail, flats. Plus, he struck me as one of those people who didn't notice clothes. He, too, was a uniform man, his style autopilot set on khakis and green plaid shirts.

"Something sprightly about you today," he said.

"Okay," I said, avoiding eye contact. I turned away and hopped in the car.

Inside, I hummed last night's *fandango*, the *cajón*'s beat reverberating inside me as if my torso housed its snare, each vibration like the moment a roller coaster hesitates before the plunge. Like that time years ago when Dan's wandering hand first traced my arm, shoulder to fingertips.

At the grocery store, I ran into Brandon Frey. I hadn't seen him since college; I'd assumed he'd moved away.

"It *is* you," he said, peeking from behind the bananas, his lips folded over in a smile like the Joker's. For a moment, I thought he wore the same oversized tweed coat he used to wear in college, but it was only a similar adult version—a way to convince himself, I suppose, he had outwitted the passage of time.

"I see you've decided to embalm yourself," he said, and chuckled. He'd always laughed at his own jokes. "You haven't changed one bit."

His face was worn out, and his posture tired, his gestures familiar but limp.

"Long time," I said, smiling politely.

"Too long." He switched his weight to the other foot in slow motion.

"Oh, well. Life. Heh. How's Lori?"

"Good. She's good. Kids are good. We're good. How's Dan?"

"Good, good. You know Dan, not a man of many demands, always happy." I shrugged.

"Lucky Dan. Good for him." He slid his hands inside the coat pockets, puffed his chest ever so slightly.

"Okay, gotta run, the cashier lines are getting longer as we speak. Five more minutes will set me back for days. Heh. Nice seeing you, Brandon."

"Good to see you."

We hugged. He lingered a tad too long. It felt like an extended pause at the end of a measure, a self-indulgent *fermata*, but then we parted and I curbed the paranoia. Besides, I needed to face a more pressing conundrum: this week's choice of probiotic.

I was already deep into the dairy aisle, trying to decide between sheep and goat yogurt when I felt a light touch on my shoulder. I turned.

"Actually, it's not good," Brandon said. "It's not good at all. Lori . . ." He looked aside, unable to look me in the eye. Then he lifted his gaze, inhaled like he was gathering strength. "She's gotten cynical. Chauffeurs the kids all the time, became a health freak. God forbid she misses yoga. Where does that leave me? Us?" His hands in pockets flared the coat open like an undone tarp. His lips were chapped, and saliva had built a white, sticky sediment in the corner of his Joker mouth. "And you seem so full of life. Fresh, radiant."

Radiant? My *cajón*-energized viscera must have been manifesting on the outside. That, or I'd mindlessly applied tinted moisturizer this morning.

"Do you have a few minutes to grab coffee and talk more?" he went on. "Catch up."

My thumb reached to fiddle with my wedding ring, an anxious gesture, but it wasn't there. I looked at my hand in horror before I realized I'd forgotten to put it back on after the gig. I knew it wasn't lost, merely displaced, but it wasn't where it was supposed to be.

"I don't know," I babbled. "It was really good to see you. But I need to pick up my kids to take the older one to her gymnastics practice and the younger one to the dentist, and then later I have yoga."

I'd forgotten what it felt like to be hit on. Out of practice on how to act cool and unruffled, I was happily out of the hunter-huntee demographic, and it was a welcome riddance. Nowadays, I reserved my energy for fighting with Dylan over plate organization in the dishwasher or explaining to Lily the otherwise commonsense impulse to close cabinet doors upon retrieving what one needed.

Brandon took a peach from his cart and bit into it. Juice trickled down his chin to his neck and under his sweater. He grinned, gave me a *this-is-not-over-yet* look, and walked away. After I made sure he was not lurking behind the shelves, I opened the dairy fridge and checked myself out in the glass door. I *did* look good. As good as anyone would in the vagueness of a glass reflection, sure, but enough to reassure me that Brandon wasn't being creepy; he was simply stating the facts. *Right on, sexy mama.*

I drove to the dry cleaner, flamenco blasting on max. The college kid who worked at the cleaner was kind of weird, but today I looked forward to his downcast mumbles. I piled Dan's dirty shirts on the counter and rested my left hand on top for a moment. He looked at it for a second, then grabbed my hand and looked straight into my eyes. I looked back, noticing the pond-like mystery and youthful resolve in his gaze.

"You have amazing skin," he said.

"Thanks." I slid my hand out of his.

"It's stirring to feel the glow of a well-preserved woman," he added in a radio voice, enunciating without affectation, which made his odd line feel somehow appropriate. His lips looked succulent, and I suddenly felt parched.

I looked away and then back at him. He no longer looked like a moping college kid high on weed and low on manners and self-confidence. Once an unacknowledged piece of airport art, his presence was now a wonderland of spellbinding detail: his Neanderthal bone structure, the regal mandible, his freckles strategically understated to amplify the allure. His toned forearms leaned on a copy of *A Movable Feast*. He must have been immersed in it before I showed up with a tan line in place of my wedding ring. A current flashed from my big toes to the back of my sinuses. I couldn't get the hell out of there fast enough.

What was with all the compliments? Had the men read some overnight memo women weren't privy to? The ever evolving rules of seduction evidently claimed collateral damage; these uncanny lines made men sound like misfits at best and, at worst, aspiring serial killers.

At home, I abandoned the groceries and rushed into the closet to find the jacket I had worn last night. I unzipped the pocket and sighed in relief when I felt my ring inside. I took it out, eager to put it back on, but the tarnished gold stared at me, dull and unkempt. I scurried to the kitchen, pulled out the stainless steel cleaner, polished the ring. I hoped that as soon as the patina was gone, the tormenting questions would leave me alone and let me resume my glorious, boring life.

When I put it on, the ring's gleam nearly blinded me. I closed my eyes and felt it with my thumb. It was there, not going anywhere. My breathing returned to normal.

* * *

I PUT THE ZITI in the oven and turned on the timer. The Unity Mutual data awaited my expert analysis. I read through the transcribed consumer interviews. Turned out, loyalty was fluid, a shapeshifter assuming whatever meaning anyone gave to it. For some, it was all about conscience, an intrinsic moral compass. For others, loyalty was flexible, at the mercy of external forces and cultural conditioning.

I glanced at the *cajón* I'd borrowed from Raiz. My thoughts drifted to what I read about it and the African slaves who defied their masters' orders by sitting on the boxes they were meant to stack. Instead, their spread legs kept the boxes in place and their hands beat the front boards, breathed life into wood. They turned boxes into drums. Was finding release a violation of rules or an expression of agency? Was Paco de Lucía loyal to the *cajón*'s inventors? Did he improve or violate it when he inserted the string in its cavity to make it a snare drum? Was he loyal to the flamenco—the form that elevated him to planetary fame—when he introduced *cajón* into the traditional lineup? Did the change add richness or diminish the true substance of the art form? Was it *cajón* that tainted the purity of flamenco, or was it the old ways that dulled its luster?

Was I disloyal when I took my wedding ring off? It hadn't led to anything questionable, but was I essentially waving to all the virile men out there with my bare ring finger and letting them know my enticing yoga-sculpted waist-to-hip ratio wasn't locked up anymore?

The questions, at first tame, snowballed into a thunderous avalanche, like a hand hitting the *cajón* front and center, feverish with repeated impact. The speed and tension piled up like those wooden boxes the slaves decided they'd no longer pile but dismantle, beat into submission, redefine, liberate.

The timer went off, the ziti bubbled. I turned on the broiler and sat on the *cajón* in front of the lit-up oven. I hit it, caressed it. My fingers and palms burned, my eyes set on ziti, watching that the sizzle didn't turn to char.

* * *

THE NEXT MONDAY, WE played Corrida again. I wore a floral skirt and when I rode the *cajón*, the skirt rose to my thighs. We played the same set list, but we sounded better this time. Raw. Feral. I'd left my wedding ring at home, tucked it in to sleep in a pouch with teeth-whitening trays.

"I told you; it's different." Flannel Crocs had brought a friend, Shearling Bomber. That baby was there again, clapping from a stroller, her smiling parents waving to me. In the middle of the floor a few tables were pulled together for a group of suits and loosened ties shooting tequila, the air warm with *patatas bravas*.

Tuesday—grocery store and dry cleaner again. Except this Tuesday was also a day of scientific pursuit. At the store, Brandon stood by the bananas. I tensed a little, thinking back to his protracted hug. My memory was now even adding a faint moan to it, but I reminded myself that memory reconstruction is malleable and unreliable. No matter the discomfort, real or imagined, I wasn't going to forfeit my grocery day without a fight; it took a year to perfect my weekday routine.

Not to mention the higher cause: I needed to confront him in the name of science, to test my hypothesis in the wild. Is the wedding ring like the on/off switch, unleashing and corralling, emboldening and inhibiting? If so, then it is like the green side of the wooden cylinder at the Brazilian barbecue that signals to the server you are still hungry, that you want more meat . . . or like a traffic light without the yellow: no transition, no second thoughts, no questions asked, on the market or off.

Brandon lit up as soon as he caught my gaze.

"You're back," he said as if catching me buying groceries meant changing my mind about meeting him for coffee, and who knows what else.

"It's my grocery shopping day," I said, careful to keep my tone neutral. Safe behind the shopping cart, right hand on the cart handle, and my left holding onto my purse strap high up in order to display the blinding gold of my polished wedding ring, I was ready to laser his irises if he dared try anything silly. He squinted and covered his eyes with the back of his palm like one does when met with some annoying kid's mirror glare.

"Lori and I are working things out," he said, his hand still a visor. "People like you inspire me to keep trying."

"Good," I said. "Have a great life, Brandon," Before he could notice me hyperventilating, I turned the corner at rice and beans.

At the dry cleaner, I took the ring off for the next phase of research. I put Dan's shirts on the counter and rested my left hand on the pile long enough for the young man to notice its ringlessness. Once he had, he looked into my eyes. Even though a part of me wanted to abort the mission, threatening to compromise the experiment, I scooped my weakness into a cold, heartless petri dish and held the eye contact. This time he didn't even bother to feed me some literary line; our locked gaze was all we needed to know that the light was green, the meat was on the market, free for all, fair game.

I was right.

But if I wriggled out of the next step, could I ever claim a guess as true insight? Intuition was all I had, and no scientist would accept a hunch as proof. I had to see the experiment through, and that meant leaning into the discomfort of empirical verification. I couldn't let a few moments of so-called loyalty—or *fidelity*, as society has contextualized it—obliterate what could be a revolutionary finding for all of humanity. To call this experiment "completed" in clean conscience, what I needed to do was not a transgression but a means to a greater scientific end. It would not even be that high of a price compared to what other scientists had to go through: archaeologists happily excavated in war zones; Marie Curie swallowed radioactive particles and welcomed death so that the rest of us could admire radium and polonium from a safe distance. What was my humble sacrifice in the face of a groundbreaking contribution to evolutionary thought? I was a courageous martyr to Science.

I took the little Casanova's hand and followed him to the back room. Out of nowhere, the beat of *cajón* rumbled in my temples. It was a deliberate *adagio* at first, gaining momentum through *moderato* and hesitating at the top, before plateauing at the menacing summit, suspended, unable to release into a drumroll before all the data were accounted for.

Our pelvises pounded into each other against the conveyor belt, ripping off winter coats and starched uniforms in a slapdash pattern. I could feel the *cajón*'s primeval rhythm overtaking my faculties. I looked across the hall at the buttoned-up shirts and wholesome quilts hanging lifeless, obedient, and boring like piled boxes, until the tempo of our flesh resurrected their sad existence into lively tremors. Possessed by the drum, I was no longer a hollow box; I could feel my inner strings, at once tense and giving, playful, fill the void with inspiration, reinvention, immortality. The quivering, plastic-embalmed clothes released the freshness of mountain springs and I had my hypothesis confirmed.

I drove home flying high on my experiment's success. I nipped the pesky voice questioning my method, swift to replace it with *Eureka!* Isn't happy mishap at the heart of a true invention? Like the discovery of penicillin, or when that scrap-metal spring fell down the stairs by accident and sprung into new life, its unsuspecting inventor uncovering the great marvel known as *Slinky*. My study not only found that men still paid attention to the ring, but that the ring needed reinvention to challenge status quo. What removes its inner tarnish, what keeps it shining, is its wearer's active engagement in novel and daring pursuits.

Dan was still a dormant drum, our marriage a neat stack of properness, a gallery of beautiful passive boxes, all checked off. For too long I'd looked at him as a piece of stable furniture, a thing not to be usurped, only dabbed with a dainty sheen, our obligatory morning and evening pecks.

I needed this ring-off-the-hand endeavor to find what I did not know I was looking for and the universe conspired to aid. There, I just made Dan a Slinky heir, a beneficiary of my bold quest for truth. But no need to boast. He can thank me after dinner, after the kids are tucked in and reading glasses folded, when the lights are dimmed and the beat of my body's drum can be unleashed.

FOR THE NEXT WEEK'S gig, I put on the knee-high boots. I hadn't worn them since the talk I gave at the Anthropological Intervention into Academic Tools and Practices Conference in Cairo years ago. The distressed cognac leather and four-inch heels created a power rim for the *cajón* as I clasped it with my calves. This time I went off the grid, played a *bulería*, added boot taps to the side boards, my body convulsing with Raiz's twelve-beat *palmas*.

Cheer. Laughter. Applause.

"You guys did it," Joe yelled over the boisterous Corrida, full on a Monday, as he brought us tequila shots. "Or I should say *you* did it, rocket woman." He clinked his glass with mine.

Rocket. I couldn't have put it better myself.

The next day, I put the boots on and went grocery shopping. The domination that burned through my core was no match for ballet flats. My ring was on to tame the flame lest it scorch the shopping list to ashes or mislead Brandon. If he still dared accost me.

He didn't show. The grocery-shopping day, mine. I reached into my purse and resurrected a neglected lipstick, ox blood 007, from the stale Goldfish graveyard at the bottom of the bag. I propped the dairy fridge door with my knee, the glass now reflecting power in high definition, parted my lips, smeared them with victory.

In the car I debated whether to keep the ring on or off before going into the dry cleaners. The *cajón* inside me simmered, pulsed the steady, nimble sinus rhythm of a completed project, a job well done.

I left the ring on. The boy shunned its glimmer. The invitation of the ringless hand was gone. He didn't seem shaken, merely reacquainted with the old reality as he punched his flat-lined disappointment into the cash register.

"Twenty-one seventy-nine," he said, like every Tuesday.

"I use the Indian hemp hand cream," I said.

"Okay," he said without looking up.

"I thought I'd let you know in case you wanted to work on the glow of a well-preserved man," I said.

"Cool," he said.

I took Dan's clean shirts and went home to make a meatloaf.

The Wife

Charlotte Edsall

I am pressed hard
back arched against the sky—
I am pushing for new birth
I am giving escape my every effort

This body stopped feeling like mine
a long time ago
I saw hands where they didn't—
where they don't belong

I saw whole cities fall
to ruins, to ash
my heart is a pillar of salt—
I don't care

I'd look again to see their children crying
because you can't
because you, *Lord*
turn your face from what you have done

Cowered—
and breaking under the weight of their lives
my family leave me here—more dust amongst rubble
they run

On the Descent

Vanessa Baehr-Jones

I REORDERED MY LIFE ON MOUNT KILIMANJARO.

I'd left for Africa shortly after graduating law school. As part of my final assignment for an international human rights clinic, I was scheduled to attend a week-long workshop on Kenya's Sex Offenses Act at a fancy conference center in the Great Rift Valley. For four days, I served as a scribe, furiously typing up whatever the government brass and Western NGO types said during hours of breakout sessions.

At night, I marveled at the sky. I had never seen the stars before, not really, not like this, with the white belt of the Milky Way tightening the universe around me, pulling me into other galaxies far above me. I found myself lost in its vibrancy, shocked at the vivid night world that I had missed all my life.

After arriving back in Nairobi, I hopped on a bus to Tanzania, impulsively deciding to tack on a side trip to climb Kilimanjaro. The international human rights lawyers at the workshop had assured me this was an entirely safe and practical thing to do. I realized only later their perspective on risk may have been skewed from decades of field work in various remote and war-torn regions of the globe.

Our fixer in Nairobi drove me down to the bus terminal and handed me off to a guy he knew who was driving a busload of passengers across the border. While everyone else in my law school class started bar prep, I would climb the highest mountain on the continent of Africa. I sat smugly in the bus with my Lonely Planet guide to Eastern Africa, thumbing through the chapter on Mount Kilimanjaro.

I thought the bus would take me to a mountain base town called Moshi, so I spent the afternoon highlighting guest houses and tour companies I found there in my guidebook. Sometime after dark, though, I heard from the only other Westerner on the bus, a college girl from England even more hapless than me, that we were destined for Arusha. The girl had lost her wallet and all her money somewhere in Kenya, and so, arriving in Arusha after dark we decided to pair up and find our way to an ATM.

Teams of taxi drivers descended on the bus when we stopped, yelling at us in English, "Good price, you come with me."

I made a split-second decision that we would have to trust in our chain of connections. My fixer in Nairobi had entrusted me to the bus driver, and now, we would ask him to entrust us to a taxi driver he knew. I approached him and told him the situation.

The girl, Charlotte, and I would need to drive immediately to an ATM, after dark, in a city we had never been before. Could he recommend a driver who would take us there?

He looked at us, a flicker of understanding in his eyes, and nodded. Leaning out of the bus, he beckoned toward the back of the crowd for a middle-aged man with a face that looked like it had seen everything.

Stepping off the bus, I pretended to ooze confidence I did not feel. I grabbed Charlotte's hand and pulled us through the crowd. Reaching the back, I extended my hand to this man in greeting, shaking his with vigor, determined to convey strength.

Once inside the quiet of his car, I leaned across the divide between the front and back seats. "We need to go to a Barclay's," I said without a trace of emotion, referring to the bank that all the Westerners used for cash. I knew this request would leave us alone, at night, with just this man and his car, as we pulled piles of cash from an ATM. It was risky, but there seemed to be no other good options.

"Right, we go," he said only.

He drove us down side streets, pitch black in the night, winding the car through a densely packed city long asleep. We pulled through the high gates of the bank that separated its fancy stone exterior from the thick trees, dirt streets, and wooden-sided houses that seemed haphazardly erected all around.

We stopped and I knew this was the moment when our trust would be tested. I reached for Charlotte's hand.

"Get out with me," I told her, thinking we should stay together.

We stood in the darkness, one light shining down on the ATM. I had used my last bills at the border when the guards had demanded a fee for entry, applicable only to Westerners, of $100. I had looked in my money belt then and pulled out the only currency I had left, remarkably exactly the amount needed, a one-hundred-dollar bill. Now, I had nothing.

I inserted my American bank card, punched in the PIN, and waited an awful minute for the machine to connect over miles of fiberoptic cables. Then, with a whirring noise, the machine spat out a series of Tanzanian bills. I grabbed the cash and raced for the car.

"Get in," I called to Charlotte. We slammed the doors, and I automatically pushed the lock down on mine. The driver waited for our instruction, not driving us anywhere yet. I sighed in relief. He had not driven off with our cash, or worse, with us. We could trust him now, I figured.

I told the driver we needed to find a safe guesthouse to stay the night. When we got there, I tipped him generously and asked him to return in the morning. I would need a guide to climb Kilimanjaro, I said. And I would need a lot of gear. The chain of trust would continue the next morning, when he would arrive at the guesthouse with Julius, my guide.

I divvied the rest of the money up with Charlotte and we purchased two rooms for the night. She would get a Western Union transfer in the morning and leave on safari. I would never see her again.

That night, I lay awake and listened to the sounds of this new city, the mosquito netting creating a protective cocoon around me, wondering if I had made a horrible mistake in coming here by myself.

MY FIRST, AND PERHAPS only, good decision on the trip was adding a rest day to my planned itinerary. I had been determined to make the climb in five days to save an extra day of paying for a guide and a team of three porters and a cook. If I were going to eat up part of my law firm bonus on a trip up Mount Kilimanjaro—an irresponsible luxury given the mountain of student loans that awaited me—I figured I should at least try to be frugal.

Halfway up the mountain, though, I decided to stop.

The first two days had gone well enough. Julius and I talked incessantly. Exchanging our life stories seemed only natural given the setting: two strangers walking alone together up one of the greatest mountains on earth. (The porters and cook ascended a more direct side route.)

The first night's huts, quaint and serviceable, were clustered in a lush green clearing amid climate zone two, the rain forest. Monkeys screeched in the brambles as I stumbled to the bathrooms to clean up for the night. Inside, large spiders spun elaborate webs from the wooden beams above me. I was so entranced by my surroundings that I almost didn't notice the first piece of bad luck on the climb.

I had unexpectedly gotten my period.

After much internal debate, I decided to suck up my dignity and ask for Julius's help. I marched down to the porters' quarters where I found Julius laughing with a group of men before a large bonfire. I pulled him aside and attempted to impart discreetly my new need for sanitary napkins. My efforts did not work. Finally, I enlisted the cook and began to explain using gestures and pointing wildly at the bathrooms what I needed.

To his credit, Julius only smiled slightly when he figured out my conundrum. He told me not to worry. A porter would be dispatched down the mountain that evening and would meet us at the rest spot the following night. Would I be OK until then?

I nodded, though I wasn't sure. I immediately went around and took up a collection from all the women I could find at the camp. By the end of the night, I had secured only one tampon to get me through a day of hiking.

The next morning, I raced ahead of Julius, embarrassed to discover at our first stop that blood was already overflowing onto my underwear and shorts. Despite the cold, I wrapped my jacket around my waist and practically ran through the next climate zone.

Behind me, Julius kept yelling, "Pole, pole!" I could hear the worry in his voice, but I did not slow down. "Slow, slow," was the key to climbing Kilimanjaro without suffering from terrible altitude sickness. I would soon pay the consequences for not heeding his call.

The altitude froze me first, though, before stealing my breath.

By the afternoon, the cold forced me back into my jacket. I trailed behind Julius as we finished the last miles of the day's hike, not wanting to be seen from behind. I could only hope my dark pants hid the disaster below.

At last, we entered a campsite that appeared wind-blown and desolate compared with the tropical camp of the night before. The stone huts sat among a barren, rocky clearing. We had long passed the tree line. Julius led the way to my hut for the night. Inside, it was windowless with rickety wooden doors, a wooden plank for a bed, and no discernable source of heat.

"Perhaps, I should take a rest day here," I turned and said to Julius before we parted for the night.

"Yes, yes," he replied. "This is a good idea. It will help you, so you can make it to the top." He knew how much I wanted to summit.

It was decided then, I would take a rest day in this windy, desolate spot.

The only warm place in the camp was the large, alpine-style lodge that sat near the edge of the clearing and overlooked the valley below. It was there that I waited alone, frozen, and wordless, for the cook to come with the sanitary napkins.

I remember watching him as he ran up the final length of path and spotted me just inside the glass of the lodge. He hurried in with the largest plastic bag of pads I had ever seen. The pads themselves were the monstrous kind, pillows of absorbent cotton.

He grinned at me as he held out the bag, triumphant in his one-day trek down and back up half the mountain. As I took the bag from him, I burst into tears. My wails echoed freely off the high wood-beamed ceiling of the lodge. I didn't bother to look around to see whether I'd disturbed any other hikers. I had no embarrassment left.

That night, I tried to clean up in the outdoor outhouse. At 11,000 feet, the water felt like a glacial stream as it hit my skin. Yet the feeling of being clean after a day soaked in my own blood was rejuvenating. Afterwards, I snuggled into the alpine sleeping bag I'd rented from a street vendor in Arusha, a clean pad snug between my thighs, and felt relief.

All my hiking gear had been acquired hastily over my first frantic morning with Julius, just two days before our trek up Kilimanjaro began. As I'd wriggled into snow pants over my shorts and pushed my bare arms through dusty down jackets, I'd hoped the clothes would work in the unknown frozen temperatures atop the mountain.

That night, at 11,000 feet, I wore every undergarment I'd brought, two layers of long underwear underneath fleece pants. The wind whipped through the uninsulated, unheated hut, sounding like a forlorn and inhuman cry. Finally, I slept.

In the morning, only the porter's light rap on the hut's door, signaling he'd left a bowl of hot water outside, could tear me out of the warmth of my sleeping bag. A couple of splashes and the water soon turned cold. I rushed half-awake down to the lodge where I knew a warm fire would greet me.

I spent the rest day journaling, playing cards with strangers, and asking everyone I could why they were climbing. A Norwegian woman in her thirties had lost her father right before the trip but decided to come anyway to remember him, she told me with tears in her eyes. There were couples on adventures, some hearty retirees, a father and his adult son. I heard from someone that far below us an entire high school football team from America was trying to ascend together.

I asked them all why they were climbing because I was looking for the answer myself.

Why was I climbing Mount Kilimanjaro? I didn't know. I didn't know anymore why I was doing anything. I had finished law school and lined up a fancy federal clerkship, but I had no idea what came next. I would be moving into the desert of the Inland Empire, to Riverside, California, where I knew no one. I would live alone again. I could already imagine the pain and uncertainty of this new life. I already ached for the companionship I suspected I would not find there. More than that, I ached to understand why I could never seem to find this connection to someone else, to a partner in life. A year from turning thirty, I wanted so badly to begin building my own family.

I left the lodge finally in the early afternoon, as the sun burned off the thick blanket of clouds that spread out below us over the valley. I walked out to the edge of the camp and stood looking out. Around me, climbers sat or stood admiring the view of the continent that opened below us.

The clouds hung like large suds on the surface of a bath, their foamy shapes gliding away to reveal the green valley below. The earth looked as far away as an undersea world and as distorted as an image through water. People and things were too far away from this altitude to be seen.

More real now were the birds who floated on expansive wings just past the cutoff to the overlook. At the edge, bits of rocks piled atop each other to form an abrupt end to the land. As I looked out, the birds glided at my level so steadily that it gave the illusion I could keep walking right off the side of the mountain and there would be some floor beneath my feet to catch me.

I stood there for a long time and envied the birds, so carefree in their mid-air dance.

When it grew too cold, I returned alone to my hut. Luckily, I had reading material. I'd brought Somerset Maugham's *Of Human Bondage* with me to Africa, but so far, had made little progress. Despite this, I'd acquired even more books, these ones Kilimanjaro-themed, at the visitor center at the base of the mountain. I don't know what I'd imagined climbing this mountain would be like—a trip to the beach? Of course, I'd also packed a journal. Weighted down with all these books, my pack had felt like lead by the end of day one, but I'd refused to let the porters carry it. Having my pack carried, I thought stubbornly, would negate the entire point of summiting.

Hemingway's *The Snows of Kilimanjaro* struck me as particularly on point—and slim—so I picked it from the pile and snuggled deep down into the sleeping bag. As the light dimmed, the slow death of the narrator became as vivid as my current reality. I could feel his fear and torment as his gangrenous leg wound turned fatal. I could imagine the vicious hubris of his safari. I could see myself slipping away from the world, now so far below me. No one even knew where I was really. And no one could come for me here, in the middle of Africa.

Of course, it was then that I began to remember a purple spot on my left thigh. How had I not thought of it before? Frantic, I pulled down the sleeping bag and my layers of undergarments to reveal a purplish-blue bulge—most likely the result of an ingrown hair, picked at until it became infected, but now it appeared to me a potentially mortal wound. Would I die up here?

The absurdity of the trip suddenly gripped me. What was I doing up here by myself? I had not trained for this. I could feel my chest getting tighter with each foot I climbed up the mountain. I had already started popping the over-the-counter altitude pills I'd bought at a pharmacy in Arusha. I had no idea what the drug was even called, whether it was regulated in the United States, or whether it would interfere with the other medications I took. But here I was, planning to summit in two days with only Julius as my guide, my medical team, and my companion. What had I done?

I slept fitfully that night. I don't recall my dreams, but I awoke with a sense of dread. When I opened the door of my hut, though, the day greeted me with bright sunshine. The air felt warmer, and I could draw in a deep breath. The rest day must have worked, I thought. My lungs seemed much more adjusted to this altitude. I would go on.

We turned toward the mountain as we set off that morning, its peak directly before us the whole day. Julius led as we rounded meandering switchbacks that, at first, seemed easier than the climb to 11,000. We would only gain 3,000 feet before we came to the next group of huts.

The air was clear, the sky a perfect blue, and I could see the snow-capped peak of Kilimanjaro. The mountain stood as a test of my will, and I felt a new determination as I faced off with it. I would summit this mountain. I would conquer the mountain as I would conquer my loneliness. I would feel no pain even as I felt only pain.

But climbing 3,000 feet at altitude proved far more difficult than I had anticipated.

By the time we stopped for the day, at just under 15,000 feet, I realized I could not breathe properly. I gasped and still felt dizzy from the lack of oxygen. Julius told me to rest, we would start out early in the morning, but it was no use. I lay on the mat in the small stone hut and could feel nothing but my heart pounding in my chest and my lungs aching for air.

I lay like that as night settled over the mountain, listening to Julius and the porters as they finished their dinner, their chatter and laughter making me feel even more alone. I willed myself to rest for what was still ahead, but I could not sleep. Tears trickled down my cheeks. Finally, I gave up and popped a bunch of the altitude sickness pills.

At two in the morning, Julius came into the hut to get me, with an apologetic look and a cup of steaming tea. Discouraged perhaps by my performance ascending through climate zone four, the highland desert zone, he had decided to start us on the summit an hour earlier than normal.

I had not been sleeping when he entered. Instead, I was now panting. My breath came in bursts, pressing down on my chest so that I couldn't lie comfortably in any position, even though every muscle in my body ached for rest. Day four's climb had been excruciating—the pack suddenly feeling as heavy as a person hanging from my back, trying to tackle me before I could reach the summit.

Who was I pulling against? And what was still propelling me forward? I had no idea, but I could not stop.

I got up and popped another pill, hoping it would ease whatever pressure was squeezing my organs in time for me to summit. I had one more day before the team I had hired—Julius, my cook, and the three porters—were scheduled to turn around and head back to the valley.

I had to summit. I would do anything to summit.

The dark night outside the hut greeted me, silent and cold. Climate zone five seemed deadly in its calm disregard for human habitation. Before us, like a tower of gray stone, rose the scree. It appeared almost perpendicular to the ground and entirely unclimbable.

The thin, frozen air filled my lungs as I gulped and panted. I gasped for air, but the chill breaths brought nothing but poison, switching my organs into a slow shutdown. My heart flitted like a trapped hummingbird.

My stomach rebelled first. I hunched over myself with the first heave, my pack swinging up and pushing down on the back of my head until I thought I would topple forward. Before I could, Julius had grabbed the top strap of my pack and was yanking me up. He patted the top of my head as yet another heave escaped me, burning the back of my throat with the taste of bile. My ears rang from the pressure of the altitude and my heart scampered like a frightened animal. My playlist for the summit slammed a loud, techno beat into my ears.

I dangled over the gray pebbled ground and watched the orange and red fluids I had released land like a Pollack painting on this moonscape of a canvas. We had reached the fifth distinct climate zone of the mountain, the arctic zone, and the pebbly gravel that carpeted the steep cliff before us had its own name, scree. Loose, with the consistency of sand, scree had to be climbed in the early morning hours when the frost had hardened it just enough for a methodical and slow switchback ascent up the rim of the cratered peak of Mount Kilimanjaro.

Now, suspended over the scree, I noticed my vomit had projected out in front of my worn, second-hand boots, leaving them amazingly unsoiled.

The bursts of vomiting emptied me. With each heave, I felt my gut releasing a toxic heaviness until I was just as thin as the air around me at 15,000 feet. I righted myself and finally felt free from what I'd left below.

"Let's go. I'm ready—I feel great," I called out.

"Do you want to lead?" Julius asked.

"No, you just go," I said. "I will follow." He stood looking at me for a moment, his face concerned.

"I will keep up," I assured him. "You just set the pace. I'll keep up." I could tell from his long pause that he was expecting to hoist me up the final ascent, but he turned finally and began the slow and steady climb.

We made our way to the base of the scree. At the foot was a small, barely visible dent in the dirt that marked the start of our path. The thin line of a trail rose along the crater's face in a large zigzag. As soon as we started, though, I stopped looking up at the mountain. Soon the hut at the base camp disappeared into the dark night. All that existed were the backs of Julius's legs in front of me, his black snow pants, and the bright white lines of his Adidas sneakers flashing against the grey scree.

Up and up we went, trudging onward, the movement becoming rhythmic and hypnotic. The music pounded in my ear, and I became one with the beat of my steps. Every step carefully placed in the exact foothold that Julius left. I refused to register the existence of anything above me or anything below. When Julius stopped, I stopped. When Julius drank, I drank. We did not speak. I did not think.

The night passed like this. Without knowing when any goal would be reached, any mountain summited, any pain ended, my mind seemed to dip into eternity. I merely existed to walk, to move. It was freeing, this existential separation from myself. There was no wondering, or questioning, just pure movement, and pure pain.

WE SUMMIT IN DARKNESS, beating the other climbing groups by an hour or more. Running along the side of the mountain like a glowing snake, I can see the faint, bouncing lights of their helmet flashlights as they ascend.

The silence of the empty peak is broken by the pounding of my heart. I can feel my heartbeat even in my face, my heart exerting itself to pump the blood through my cheeks, my lips, even my eyeballs. I can hear the pulse in my ears, drowning out Julius's voice as he mouths something at me, his face focused now in alarm.

I have dropped my walking poles and they dangle from my wrists. A thought slowly begins in my head as I stand there motionless, but I can't seem to communicate the words to my mouth. Finally, I manage to pull my frozen lips open. "I can't feel my hands."

Julius acts immediately, ripping off my gloves, pulling up his jacket, and shoving my hands against the warmth of his bare stomach. I smile in gratitude, my every thought reduced to momentary physical needs. Physical pain, physical pleasure—the only experiences I can register.

We stand there for a moment, but he tells me to keep moving.

"We must keep moving until we're down the mountain," he yells at me. "Would you like me to take your picture at the summit?"

He smiles then. Summiting is the moment that doubles his team's tips. He also knows how much I've yearned for this mark of achievement.

I stumble back and unzip my pocket where I've kept my phone and pass it to him. We walk side by side toward Uhuru Peak, as if toward an altar, my mind now focused on the idea that I might have a heart attack. The wailing of my heartbeat roars like a siren pounding through my body in warning.

I pose with two peace signs, a leftover habit from sightseeing in China.

Looking back at the photo, years later now, the darkness almost overwhelms the young woman, alone in the center, standing next to a wooden pole of old signs demarking the highest point on the continent of Africa. Still, her brightness seems to fight back. From head to toe, her body is encased in a neon yellow snow jacket and pants. She's smiling, of course. Always smiling. Even as her heart bursts.

I did not find anything there on top of Mount Kilimanjaro. I certainly didn't find myself. I felt only the cold darkness before the sunrise, and death chasing at my heels.

No, I found what I had come for on the descent.

He grabs my arm and pulls me after him. When we reach the edge of the scree, the mountain dipping into an abyss before us, he stands me in front of him, grabs me around the waist, and lines my feet in front of his. He pushes us forward and I feel gravity give way as we float, gliding down the scree like alpine skiers, the dirt loosening to dust under our boots.

The summit releases us.

The day breaks over the mountain, the peak in front of us suddenly silhouetted against a softening blue sky. The sun appears in slanting rays that grow sharper with each foot we descend.

The descent frees my body and my mind. In place of pain, I feel the warmth of Julius behind me and the sunlight bathing my face. I breathe and my lungs fill again. Life. I can feel it completely as my body thaws and my heart slows. And it feels marvelous just to be alive. To breathe and to live.

WE CAME DOWN THE mountain in one day; with each step my body awoke to the world in a new feeling of gratitude. Yes, my body seemed to shout as I greeted the warmth and humidity that clung to the air in climate zone two. Yes, my lungs burst with deep inhales of the air around me. Yes, my mind glided forward down the descent, reflecting on all the steps yet to come in my life and believing now that I could accomplish them.

I had survived this mountain. I had survived it all. I would survive whatever lay ahead.

Over the last few miles, we passed the American football team as they began their ascent. Every five yards or so, another clump of students and chaperones would pass me, and I would raise a hand in greeting and call out in my American-accented English, "Good luck!"

By the time we reached the bottom, I'd narrated my journey up the mountain several times to different clumps of the football team, doling out advice about rest days and altitude sickness with a warmth that felt impossible just a few days ago. They felt like a family, all those fellow Americans climbing together, and I felt like a part of their family in my own way.

Riding back to Arusha in the back seat of the SUV, wedged in between two of my porters, I took swigs from the bottle of hard grain alcohol they passed back and forth to Julius in the front. Laughing and drinking with them, the alcohol ripping through me like lightning with each gulp, the warm gusts from the valley floor balmy and tropical, I felt so close to these men, like there existed no boundary between my laughter and theirs. Summiting or not summiting seemed irrelevant now. What mattered was this feeling—this end to my loneliness.

I swore then that I would close this distance between myself and the world. Whatever fear had pushed me into the closed-off sound booth of my life, stranding me in my own form of human bondage, I would conquer it. I would find a way to be close to people again. For this—this intoxicating feeling of laughter and sweaty skin pressed to mine—was happiness.

THAT NIGHT, AT A beer garden in Arusha, Julius asked me to marry him. He knew me so well by then that he told me everything I wanted to hear: He would move back to Hawaii with me, we could live there and have children together. I would never be alone again.

I hated myself then for forgetting in my blissful descent the realities of the men who had helped me up the mountain. I had entered their lives, a privileged and entitled Westerner, and climbed their continent's greatest mountain on a whim, only succeeding because of their hard work. How blind had I been in my mission to conquer my own demons, like so many white people before me?

I gave in and kissed him that night outside of my guesthouse, but I did not invite him in. He was the kind of man who could walk away and still turn back with a smile and one last wave.

As I watched him leave, I realized that I loved Julius in the way a person loves someone who has just saved their life. Marriage to me presented an opportunity to him for a better life, and I felt horrible that this was the way the world worked. Yet a part of me also felt grateful that even given these strange dynamics, he still wanted me, he could still envision a life with me, even children with me.

I knew that I could not marry him. We were from two different worlds and mine was calling me back. I would fly home to America alone, but I would never forget him, or the feel of his arms gripping me from behind as we descended the mountain fused together. And I would never forget the promise of that descent: life.

What if We Were Named After What We Bring Each Other?

fenestra

Jesus is a Black woman
I'll let that sink in . . .
Jesus is a Black Woman
she lives on the street
outside the Laundromat
on University Ave
This is not an abstract concept
this is reality, not metaphor
insight, not reason
This information is valid even if
you disagree
Her dog's name is Bible
he is a Chihuahua mix
he is tethered to her ankle
She calls him her comfort animal
Jesus just wants a phone
a ride
a bathroom
cigarettes
someone to talk to
someone to walk with

She calls them a word I cannot say
—the White folk, the Black folk, the Brown folk—
the ones who threw her out
the ones who pass her by
everyday
Every. Day.
She hates Des Moines
She says it doesn't want her
She says it doesn't have her

Jesus is proud of her name,
proud to christen herself
She says she deserves it
Says she is slave to no one
She smells of human skin and Kool Lite 100s
$10 a pack
$10 a *fucking* pack
She pays with her own money
Jesus wants to live forever
but not on the curb
She says you don't have to kill anything to live
She says to die is to burn
She does not want to burn
Jesus is a Black Woman
Do you understand?
She calls me Water because I brought her water
but what would she have called me yesterday?
and what will she call me tomorrow?

Vessels of Light

Sandra L. Meade

Hazel Atlas
Atlas
Mason
Kerr
Ball
the transparent raised letters
on glass jars
are names for saving
a family, a season,
the vegetables, applesauce,
and the 48 oz. wide-mouth Mason
speaks of meat, maybe chicken,
but almost always, there's
a woman, knives, and a full canner
of boiling water on a wood stove.
Jars older than rural electrification,
gifted generation to generation,
now stand silent on my kitchen counter,
their wavy bubbled light
shining through. They are women
lined up, Atlas strong shouldered,
thick-bodied, transparent and ready.
A century old, clear or a light blue cast,

they hold light, preserve figures
and shapes from the past. Women
working the ground, gardening, gathering
by the turn and tilt of earth as we circle
our star making rhythms of life,
an interdependence every living
cell needs. These jar women
are from my attic, my history,
an inherited strength in our bones.

What to Expect When You're Quite Certain You Don't Want to Be Expecting

E. Marla Felcher

PROMISES.

When my seventy-year-old quadriplegic grandfather lay dying of pneumonia in a drug-induced haze, I leaned over his hospital bed, got close enough to feel his stubble, and smelled death for the first time. I did not say, *I forgive you for voting for Nixon.* I did not say, *I'll miss you every time I eat bagels and whitefish and lox.* I did not say, *I love you.* I said, *If you live I'll have a baby.* It was my final bargaining chip, a Hail Mary plea. When he died a few hours later, my first thought was, *Thank God I'm off the hook.* I was thirty years old and had been married for eight years.

Expert Advice.

For my twentieth birthday, in 1977, my mother sent me Marilyn French's just-published book, *The Women's Room*, stories of miserable suburban women slogging through the mind-dulling drudgery of housewifery and child-raising in the 1960s. Nothing but "string beans and shit," is how one of the women described her life, a phrase that left a memory stain so deep it's stayed with me all these years. Though the book was fiction, it read like an ethnography, an anthropologist's account of an exotic, faraway subculture. It was horrifying.

I grew obsessed with digging to the root of the women's misery. Partly, it was the husbands. Five days a week they doctored and lawyered and struck business deals, while their Ivy League–educated wives remained trapped at home, tending to a never-ending stream of dirty diapers and wrinkled shirts. Marrying a man who cheered my ambition would solve part of the problem. Which left the children. *Someone* had to mitigate the mothers' work, and it was not going to be me. Boring. Boring. Boring. Outsourcing to a babysitter or nanny—a stranger!—was too damn scary. How would the nanny-stranger respond when imaginary Rachel tripped and skinned a knee? Would she scoop her up and kiss the boo-boo, or tell her to get over it and suck it up? Rachel's mother should be there to pick her up. Yet, I did not have the energy to worry about anyone 24/7. And worry I would, about what was happening when I wasn't with Rachel, and when I was. "Dogs are better than kids," I'd tell anyone who'd listen, "because they don't grow up and blame you in therapy." I could conjure no solution.

I can still see my college roommate, Jan, sprawled across the bottom bunk in our dorm room, her waist-length hair pulled back into a ponytail, me on the floor in a beanbag chair, wearing patched bell-bottom jeans, occasionally reaching up to swap out records—Joni Mitchell, Bob Dylan, Carole King. I take a long draw from my beloved foot-long plastic blue bong, and hold it.

"It's the kids," I tell Jan, passing the bong. "I'll never have them."

"You'll change your mind," she said.

"Never," I said, exhaling.

"Can you name one married woman who does not have kids?" Jan asked. "*Everyone* can't be wrong."

"*Most* can be. Richard Nixon won a second term."

"You'll meet The One," she said, shaking her head, "and then you'll want a family."

How had my nineteen-year-old roommate, who didn't even have a boyfriend, become an expert on childbearing? Reading? Observation? How had I missed this?

"You'll be a great mom," Jan said with certainty. "Plucky. Your kids will be cool."

I imagined Rachel as a cool six-year-old, an unkempt, stringy-haired spitfire, who preferred blue jeans over pink tutus, and requested a magnifying glass for her birthday, to get a closer look at her shoebox collection of bugs. Then, I imagined her as a baby, a bundle of decidedly uncool needs. When women *oohed* and *aahed* over infants, asking in a high-pitched voice, "Don't you think she's adorable?," I did my best not to grimace. That I had this reaction made me odd, for a woman. That I was unwilling to hand the reins to anyone, even my own child, made me downright weird. My nightmare scenario: Rachel as an incalcitrant toddler, protesting, "You are not the boss of me!" and knowing she was right.

Battles.

When Jan and I tired of arguing, we'd watch reruns of sitcoms on her postage stamp–sized, black-and-white TV. Among our favorites was *I Love Lucy*, the chocolate factory episode. In it, Lucy and her friend Ethel stand over a conveyer belt working side by side, wrapping pieces of chocolate candy as they roll by. But the conveyor belt moves too quickly, and soon the women realize they can't grab and wrap the candies fast enough. Shoving them into their pockets, under their hats, and finally, into their mouths, Lucy turns to Ethel and says, "We're fighting a losing game."

One night, as Jan and I were watching the episode for the umpteenth time, I had a vision. Or maybe it was a daydream, I'm not sure there's a difference. It popped into my head, like a little movie. In my daydream/vision, newborn babies were moving across a conveyer belt. Naked and pink, all girls, they were lying on their backs, stretching their short pudgy arms to grab their short, pudgy feet. Standing over the conveyer belt was a plump old woman, wearing a belted black dress and red babushka headscarf, holding a wooden ruler with both hands. As each baby rolled by, the woman tapped her on the forehead with the ruler, imbuing her with a trait. Tap. Blue eyes. Next baby. Tap. Long legs. Next baby. Tap. Shy. Next baby. Tap. Curly hair. Next baby. Tap. Plays well with others. This goes on for what seems like a long time. Finally, the last baby is in front of the old woman, and she's about to tap her with the last trait: Mother. She lifts her ruler, pauses mid-air, and allows the baby to pass, untouched. Looking up, she raises her eyebrows and shrugs, as if to say, *there's nothing I can do.*

I reached over Jan and turned off the TV.

"The kid thing," I told her. "It's not my fault. I was born this way."

"But you can change," Jan said with a mournful whine. "You'll *want* to change."

I was fighting a losing game.

Poetry.

Recently, a smoke alarm battery in our kitchen began to beep. Just when the silence between the beeps was long enough to trick me into thinking maybe it was the last one, it would start again. My husband was out of town, we didn't own a ladder tall enough to reach the alarm, and it was after ten p.m., too late to knock on a neighbor's door.

I called my neighbor Gus. He laughed when I explained the problem. "What are you, a damsel in distress?" he asked, his tone somewhere between mocking and naughty. It wasn't the first time Gus had irritated me with a sexist remark, but I was in no position to call him out. "Bring a battery and a ladder," I told him.[1]

Waiting for Gus, I thought of *Mighty Mouse,* my favorite Saturday morning cartoon as a kid. It starred a man-mouse superhero who wore a yellow unitard and red Superman-like cape, flew through the air, and often was summoned to the aid of his love interest, Pearl Pureheart, a yellow-haired damsel in distress.

---

[1] If my husband had been home, I'm certain he would have called Gus more quickly than I did. I don't know what Gus would have called him, but best guess is that it would not have been damsel in distress.

I remembered one episode. In it, a mustachioed, black-caped villain with a top hat (who I now realize looked like the Monopoly man's licentious younger brother) had whisked Pearl to a dilapidated mansion and tied her to a chair. As Pearl squirmed to set herself free, a male voice-over asked in an ominous baritone, *Where is Mighty Mouse? Will he save his damsel in distress?* On cue, Mighty Mouse swooped through an open window and untied Pearl. Together they flew away, Pearl tucked safely under her savoir-beau's arm.

The term *damsel in distress* first appeared in the English language in *Sylvia's Complaint of Her Sexes Unhappiness*, a book-length verse, published in 1688. Sylvia complained at length about men behaving badly (*"Men so Artfully disguise their Passion; And call their vilest Lewdness Inclination"*), then turned her attention to *customs*, "rigid laws" that limited a woman's life options and rendered her helpless:

> The three Conditions of the Female Life
> Are *Virgin*, *Widdow*, or 'fore that, a *Wife*;
> To each of which Inexorable Stars,
> Have order'd such a weighty Load of Cares:
> So far out-ballancing our short liv'd Joys,
> The pleasure ev'n of *Living* it destroys . . .

> Hence 'tis, our Thoughts like Tinder, apt to fire,
> Are often caught with loving kind Desire;
> But *Custom* does such rigid Laws impose,
> We must not for our Lives the thing disclose.
> If one of us a *lovely Youth* has seen,
> And streight some tender Thoughts to feel begin;
> Which *liking* does insensibly improve
> It self to *longing fond impatient Love*.
> The *Damsel* in distress must still remain,
> Tortur'd and wrack'd with the tormenting *Pain* . . .

Reading the poem, my mood took a U-shape, starting high with *You go, girl!* elation, plummeting with the unsettling familiarity of Sylvia's (modern-day) complaints, then rising again with her prescription, an Rx for her sisters-in-pain: build a utopian community populated by women who vowed to *"deny their procreative function and prove their independence from men."* I'd been validated by a seventeenth-century fictional heroine.

And there was a bonus! Sylvia had proved Gus wrong, too. A damsel became distressed, *Tortur'd* and *wrack'd (with) Pain*, not waiting for a man's help, rather when she was prohibited from acting upon her desire. Stultifying gender norms distressed her, not lack of a battery or ladder, or a villain's ropes.

Personal Control.

Max was a professor, but not a real professor. He was a twenty-two-year-old business school PhD student, teaching for the first time. He told us to call him by his first name, which was easy to do since he was too young to look like anyone's idea of a professor. His outfits didn't help. No Oxford button-down shirts or wool blazers with patches on the elbows for Max; he favored spongy, blue-green plaid slacks, and clingy, Quiana (faux silk) shirts. Over six feet tall, he was so thin I could see his hip bones pushing against his pants. He wore his big, bushy hair in an Afro, and if you saw him from behind you might think he was Black, because of his hair and the Black Power Afro Pick sticking out of his back pants pocket. But he wasn't Black, he was white Jewish, like me. Later, I learned the pick had more to do with pragmatism than politics; finding a comb that could break through all of that hair was not easy.

The class was Organizational Behavior I: Leadership and Employee Motivation. With graduation less than a year away, in a post–*Women's Room* panic, I'd scrambled to add business classes to my psychology major. The housewives had clarified my career aspirations. I wanted what the husbands had, a fast-paced business career that propelled me into the world. Exactly what that career would be remained a mystery, though I imagined it would involve a burgundy leather briefcase, dark tailored suits, and sensible pumps. Enrolling in Organizational Behavioral I was a low-risk first step.

I remember only one concept from that class: equations can tame sloppy constructs, e.g., *Employee Performance = Motivation × Ability*. It was the tidbits Max shared about his personal life that caught my attention. He would graduate with his PhD the following year, then seek a (real) professor job; he was working on his dissertation, "Personal Control in Organizations"; he could memorize a fifty-digit string of numbers and recite them forward and backward; he was a highly ranked tournament bridge player.

I was smitten.

By mid-semester, I had a hunch Max was The One.

Pam, a fellow psychology major, was in Max's class with me. She wasn't interested in the subject; she'd signed up to find a future businessman husband. Her bait? Low-cut floral blouses, tight mini-skirts, copious amounts of sparkly blue eye shadow, and cherry-red lipstick. She was the only person I knew, besides my grandmother, who carried a can of Aqua Net in her purse. Once I'd confessed my crush on Max, I could not have asked for a better co-conspirator. We'd sit together toward the back of the narrow, bowling alley–ish room, and pass notes.

I wrote in loopy purple ink, "After class I want to stay and talk to him. What should I say?????"

"Boy, you've got it bad!" Pam wrote back. "Tell him to lose those metal frames and get tortoise-shell glasses."

The ethics around a quasi-professor dating a student did not occur to us; in those days, the norms (and laws) dictating academic relationships were lax.

When Max wrote a flirty message under the "A" on my midterm paper, *I'm impressed. You demonstrated your knowledge in the most interesting way I've seen in my many years of teaching at the university level!*, Pam's coaching shifted into overdrive. She laid out her plan over a cafeteria lunch.

"Look," she said, leaning so far across the Formica table that her breasts touched her sandwich. "You're always bragging about what a big feminist you are. Look at your T-shirt. The Future Is Female? I don't think so. You think my makeup is girly-girl. I think you waiting for him is worse. Ask him out."

Ask *him* out? Never would this have occurred to me. The previous summer, I'd worked as a waitress at a boardwalk diner on the Jersey Shore with my best friend Ellen, where, on our days off, we'd sit on the beach and pour over "How to Get a Teen-Age Boy and What to Do with Him When You Get Him," a best-selling guide on where to meet a guy (e.g., library, ski chalet, beach, etc.) and how to lure him into asking you out. The trick was to perfectly calibrate your flirting— bold enough to signal your interest, but not overly bold, or he'd think you were loose.[2] A girl asking out a boy? Strictly verboten.[3]

"I can't," I told Pam.

"You have to," she demanded.

I don't remember how long I waited, a day, or a week. What I remember is staying after class, watching Max pack up his notes. I remember the pretense: career advice. I remember he suggested I stop by his office hours. I remember saying, "No. How about the bar at the William Penn Hotel? Friday night." I remember my emotion, fright. I remember worrying he'd think I was a slut.

A month after that first date, Max moved in with me and my two roommates. When I graduated a few weeks after that, and we got

---

[2] The section Ellen and I found most useful was "Beachcomber's Prop Guide for Better Boy Hunting." Prop: broken sunglasses. You say to boy, "My really favorite sunglasses are broken. Could you fix them?" Boy says to you, "Sure." Special instructions: Just take a little screw out of the side of your sunglasses to break them.

[3] After writing "How to Get a Teenage Boy," author Ellen Peck went on to found the National Organization for Non-Parents (NON) in Palo Alto, CA, to advance the notion that men and women could choose not to have children—to be childfree. The organization later changed its name to the National Alliance for Optional Parenthood.

our own place, my parents gave us a set of white Corelle dishes with blue daisy trim, service for six, and my grandparents sent a full set of Revere pots and pans, as encouragement. It worked. One night, over a bottle of Mateus and a plain, extra cheese pizza at our favorite bar, I asked Max, "Do you think we should get married?" He said yes. Neither of us got down on a knee; there was no ring in a blue velvet box, no fireworks, rainbows, or background string quartet. Marriage was the logical next step. My parents threw us a wedding in their wood-paneled rec room and hired an accordion player to mill around the guests and take requests.

I was twenty-one years old, Max was twenty-three.

Now it is unfathomable to imagine a couple spending as little time discussing children as Max and I did. Work was our future, not children. What consumed us was where Max would land his first professor job, and where I'd get my MBA. Would we live together no matter what, or were we willing to commute?

Yet, once we announced our engagement, our children were very much on the minds of others.

"You'll love it," Audrey, the wife of one of Max's colleagues, told me. "Babies are like puppies, but better."

"Hurry up," said my grandfather. "I want to take my grandson fishing."

"We have plenty of time," I told everyone. By then, I'd learned this was easier than telling the truth.

Defaults.

We had an appointment with the rabbi who'd be marrying us. The night before, Max and I were in bed, watching TV. It must have been past midnight, because Tom Snyder was interviewing a guest, and he was on after Johnny Carson. Max's breathing became louder and more rhythmic as he hovered close to sleep. I nudged his shoulder.

"We need to talk about children," I said.

"What?" he murmured.

"I'm afraid of what the rabbi's going to say, the prayers."

"What prayers?"

"Be fruitful and multiply. Calling us *man* and *wife*? We need to cut him off at the pass." I sat up, cross-legged on top of the covers, and looked down at Max.

True, I'd started out being anxious about the ceremony. I'd known the rabbi for years, and he was old-school. What if he refused to make concessions? Would I capitulate? What about rice, wasn't that about fertility? And stomping on a glass—was that about kids, too? I had no idea. Staring blankly at the TV, listening to Max breathe, my worries had meandered in multiple directions, from the rabbi, to the weather (why were we getting married in March, shouldn't we have waited until summer?), and my parents (would they side with the rabbi, no matter what?), until they'd dead-ended at Max. What if he wasn't as committed to remaining child-free as I was? Sure, when a toddler wailed in a restaurant and I snarked, "Explain to me why those parents seem surprised their precious angel is ruining everyone's dinner," my future husband smiled conspiratorially and shook his head, in what I assumed had been agreement, but how could I be certain? Max was not a ruminator, he was a doer, and the question of children required joint rumination.

"It's more than the rabbi," I said. "It's kids. The ones I do not want to have."

Max reluctantly slid his torso out from under the covers and rested his back against the headboard. His eyes were droopy, the way they got when he was exhausted. He was wearing the first gift I'd bought him, a white T-shirt with Pizza Makes Me Passionate written in red letters across the chest, inside a slice of pizza.

"And?" he asked, dragging the word out multiple syllables.

"Have you ever imagined your life with a child? I mean, day-to-day, going to work and thinking about who will stay with it life, coming home late, exhausted, and having to feed it life, calling our friends to say we can't come to dinner because our babysitter just canceled life? No. Did Audrey tell *you* to have a baby because it will be better than a puppy? No. Has anyone ever said to you, *never say never, you'll change your mind, your biological clock will tick, you'll regret being childless when you're old blah, blah, blah?* No. Well, welcome to my world, because they say it me."

Max looked toward the ceiling, as if he were solving a math problem in his head. Sitting there, I watched him think. He started to say something, then stopped. I waited. I got out of bed and turned off the TV.

"Okay, here's the thing," he said while I was still standing up. "Most people set their default on children as *yes*. Everyone assumes they'll have them. Little analysis goes into the decision, because it's the default. We'll change our default to *no*, assume we won't. But if either of us ever feels an urge, we'll talk."

And at that moment I realized yet another reason Max was going to be a stellar life partner: where I saw a decision as being black and white, just two options, he could conjure an as-yet unidentified, superior third. Years later, he'd go on to become a renowned scholar, publishing hundreds of articles and dozens of books on decision-making and negotiation. As far as I was concerned, he was pretty good at both before all of that, when he was a rookie quasi-professor.

"By the way," Max said, as we both slid back under the covers, "Audrey bet me ten dollars we'd have at least one kid by the time you were thirty."

"Did you take it?"

"Of course."

And with that we put our decision to rest, where each passing year it burrowed deeper inside of us, as individuals, and together as a couple, until it was buried so deeply that it became part of our identity, increasingly difficult and inconvenient to unearth. *Marla and Max, who don't have children. Marla and Max, who don't want children. Marla and Max, who changed the default.*

Sleuths.

Over the years, friends with kids have sought (in good faith) to unravel my *why*. Their jumping-off point tends toward my mother. Was she tender enough? Nurturing enough? Patient enough? Happy enough? Did she work or stay at home? Each woman fills in the blanks with her idea of the essentials of good mothering. This is what I tell them. My mother lived *The Women's Room* life. Married at eighteen, she'd dropped out of college at twenty, when she became pregnant with me in 1956. By the time she sent me *The Women's Room*, she'd gone back to school, graduated, and was teaching American history at my high school. During this time, she discovered feminism. The same woman who had counseled thirteen-year-old me before my first date (Larry Keene, a bar mitzvah party), "Ask him questions about himself, boys don't like girls who talk too much," encouraged me to get a job pumping gas (*"It's time for women to break barriers."*) the summer I waitressed on the Jersey Shore. I may have been a victim of ideological whiplash, but I was not a victim of especially bad parenting. And here's the thing: My mother never, ever pushed children on me. I've always suspected she was jealous I had a choice.

If anyone in my family holds a clue, it's my sister, who, as a child (ages two through thirteen), threw epic, unpredictable tantrums. Anything could ignite her: my mother refusing to buy Cocoa Puffs at the A&P, my father fussing a bit too much over the A's on my report card, the stress of dressing for an extended-family holiday dinner. She'd throw herself onto the floor (our carpeted living room, or sticky supermarket linoleum) and curl her slight body into a ball so tightly you could count each bone of her spine as she rocked back and forth and moaned. At some point she'd unfurl, thrash her arms and legs, and scream unintelligible grievances. Of course, her fury had more to do with what was going on inside of her than what anyone had said or done, but I didn't know that. Often, I blamed myself. For getting A's, for usurping my parents' attention, for objecting when she borrowed my records without asking. Though she was younger than me, and scrawny to my chubby, she terrified me. *Be careful, please tell her she's the prettiest little girl in the world. Be careful, or she'll ruin Passover dinner. Be careful. Be careful. Be careful.* We tried, but often failed.

Why, then, I asked my sister repeatedly, as an adult, was she desperate to have kids?

"I had a horrible childhood, I was miserable," she'd say. "I want to do it right." This has always befuddled me.

Did my childhood play a role in my decision to not become a mother? Of course. But like any significant life event, say, cancer or divorce, there is no single causal reason, no straight line between cause and effect.

Work.

Max published his dissertation, I got my MBA, and we moved to Boston, where Max taught in Boston University's business school and I worked in the market research department at Gillette, Liquid Paper Division. My job was to predict monthly sales of white and off-white correction fluid. Those were the days before computers, when it was tougher to cover mistakes. Demand for Liquid Paper was constant; if I forecast a change of more than 10 percent in either direction, it was a big day at work. A year into this job, when my boss asked me to dress up as Big Bird for his son's third birthday party, I quit, and landed a job at a consulting firm. It came with a salary higher than Max's, a gold American Express card, and Celtics season tickets. I bought a blue Fiat convertible with a back seat just large enough for an overnight bag and my briefcase (burgundy leather).

My clients were M&M Mars and Nabisco; I built statistical models that predicted sales of candy and salty snacks. Landing at LaGuardia on the Eastern Shuttle, I'd race through the airport clutching my briefcase, suit bag strapped onto my shoulder, wending my way through slow-moving dawdlers, to reach the taxi line before everyone else. When the driver asked, "Bridge or tunnel into the city?" I had an opinion. After a full day of meetings I'd check into the

Helmsley Palace, where I'd eat room service hamburgers and drink half bottles of red wine, propped up on the bed with oversized pillows, and watch CNN. After dinner, I'd call Max and share an inside baseball client story: "The CEO's pet project is mint-flavored M&Ms, but we're predicting they'll flop." I was at the top of my game.

I remained friends with Kathy, a work pal from Gillette. She'd quit when her maternity leave was over. We met for lunch a few months after her son was born. She was exuberant, wearing her exhaustion like a badge of honor. Kathy knew how I felt about having kids; we'd talked about it over dozens of lunches. That day we joked about me trying to get her to crack—to say, *It's nothing like I thought it would be,* or at least admit she resented her consultant husband just a tiny bit for abandoning her at home five days a week with a baby.

"Nope. I love it," she told me. "I'm never going back to a mind-numbing job. We're talking about number two." And I thought, *string beans and shit.*

Hugging Kathy good-bye, when I squeezed her a bit too tightly, she loosened her arms, pushed away a few inches, looked at me, and said, "Let's stay friends," acknowledging what we both knew, that over time we'd drift. She was to become the first of my friends to replace me with women from Lamaze class, preschool playdates, and the carpool line. It made sense. I had zero interest in hearing about potty training or growth spurts, and they didn't care how long my plane had been delayed on the LaGuardia runway, or the fate of mint M&Ms. Still, it felt like a loss.

Questions.

1. *How many children do you have?* is a safe conversation opener, petty small talk—but only if the woman on the receiving end answers with an integer greater than zero. I have two answers at the ready. If I'm feeling cranky, or not in the mood to engage, I'll answer *none,* and leave it at that. My failure—refusal—to elaborate puts the onus on the inquisitor to get out of the mess she now realizes she's got herself into.

If I'm feeling chatty, or suspect the person is someone I'd like to know, I give her more. I tell her how long Max and I have been married (proving *I have a long-term partner*), confiding that we never wanted kids (proving *choice, not reproductive failure*), ending with a heartwarming story of the most recent girls' trip I'd taken with my niece Yu Lin, to Hershey Park or, for her sixteenth birthday, to Paris (proving *there are children in my life whose company I enjoy*). Rarely does anyone ask a follow-up question; doing so would require wading into fraught waters.

2. *Because you couldn't or because you didn't want to?* Shortly after my fiftieth birthday, I was seated at a dinner party next to a man well into his eighties, a long-retired gynecologist. His daughter, a theater producer, had recently hit it big on Broadway. He had every right to be proud, but after regaling me with stories about her childhood, high school years, and pre-famous young adulthood (*we knew from the start she'd be a star!*), I stopped paying attention to the content and focused on his punctuation, eager for a comma or period, so I could excuse myself to the bathroom. He didn't stop until our hostess placed a dish of ice cream and berries in front of each of us. Then, he picked up his spoon and took a hard look at me, as if he'd just realized there was someone on the other end of his conversation.

"So, how many children do you have?" he asked.

"None," I told him, sliding a spoonful of ice cream into my mouth.

"Because you couldn't, or because you didn't want to?"

Staring at the old gynecologist, I closed my lips into a tight, horizontal line, like a neutral-faced emoji, intending to stare this man down, to signal it was not okay to have asked me that. Did he think I was his patient, a woman to fix? I cleared the ice cream from my throat, put down my spoon, and excused myself. On the way to the bathroom, I mumbled under my breath, "Why did you have them? Was your daughter planned, or was she a mistake?"

3. *Do you regret not having children?* Last week I got an email from an old high school friend, a woman I hadn't heard from in years. She'd

been the smartest friend I'd had, great at science and math. Her email brought me up to date on the last decade or so of her life. She taught environmental sustainability at a local college, babysat for her six-year-old grandson, visited her daughter, who's at NYU in graduate school, and her son, who was working on his PhD in Georgia. Her mother (who had paid my friend to lose weight when we were kids, $1 a pound), was in assisted living, with dementia. Unremarkable middle-age catch up.

It was my old friend's closing question that got me. *I'm curious, did you ever have any regrets about not having children?*

My impulse was to return her impertinence, as I'd fantasized doing with the gynecologist. *I'm curious, did you ever have any regrets about having any of your children? If so, which one(s)?* But I didn't, because I had nothing but fond memories of this woman, and, if I'm being honest, still felt indebted to her for letting me copy her geometry homework in tenth grade.

I typed *No!* and hit reply.

Travel.

My sister called to ask me to go to China, to pick up Yu Lin, the fifteen-month-old daughter she and her husband were adopting. Their four-year-old biological son, whom she'd had at forty, would stay home with his father, and she didn't want to go alone.

The trip required spending two weeks in country with an adoption group of twelve strangers, the first week in Beijing, bureaucratic, without the children, the second week in Nanchang, bonding with them.

Listening to my sister describe the logistics, I thought of Francine Prose's, *Guided Tours of Hell*, a novella that follows a group of self-absorbed academics assembled for the First International Kafka Congress in Prague, as they convene for lectures, meals, and tours of former concentration camps. Then, I thought of my sister spending a week alone in a hotel room with a traumatized toddler.

"I'll think about it," I told her.

"I need to know this week," she said.

Max questioned my sanity. Nothing good would come of it, the parents would drive me nuts, I'd be bored by their conversations, lose my mind in the midst of so many kids.

"I'll be an anthropologist, an embedded observer," I explained. "My sister's sick of my *why* questions, this will increase my sample size."

"Promise you will *not* share a room," he said, knowing I'd already made up my mind. "You'll need an escape."

The only person in favor of the trip was Jimmy, my forty-something mailman, a Chinese immigrant. Multiple times a week he'd ring my doorbell, ostensibly to hand-deliver my mail, but primarily to share and collect gossip. He hated that Max and I had a house big enough for children, yet we used the two extra bedrooms for offices. Now, he had hope.

"Oh, when you see those babies you will bring home one, maybe two," Jimmy predicted. "Chinese make good children!"

THE FIRST WEEK, WE saw Beijing through the smeared windows of a van, as we were shuffled between government buildings to sign forms and hand over wads of cash. I came to appreciate the satisfying thud of a rubber stamp.

Our group spent evenings in the hotel restaurant, sharing Lazy Susan meals of oily Chinese greens and chicken in glutinous white sauce. After dinner, we'd decamp across the lobby to the hotel bar to drink scotch and Tsing Tao beer. Inevitably, the conversation would turn to stories of reproductive failure, dashed hopes, and gratitude for this one last chance. The strength of the couples' fortitude was impressive; the universe had told them again and again they could not have children, yet they would not give up. I tried to think of something, anything, I didn't have that I wanted as much as these people wanted a daughter, and came up blank.

I was a terrible anthropologist. The soon-to-be parents talked excitedly about their future, not their past, and certainly not what I was after, the *whys. Why do you find your life unsatisfying without a child? Why have you hinged your happiness on a Chinese orphan?* Face-to-face with their naked, raw hope, I couldn't find the words to ask. Mostly I hung back, becoming increasingly comfortable with my outsider status, the childless supportive sister.

Finally, it was "Gotcha Day." The orphanage, a white Stalinist building straight out of a Cold War movie, had a parking lot the size of a Walmart superstore. By the time we arrived, the spaces closest to the building had been taken by vans identical to ours. Dozens of adoption groups had been in Nanchang all week, and now we'd come together for a single purpose, to pick up the girls. As our driver parked the van, I whispered to my sister, "Are you okay?" She slapped my hand and whispered back, "Sshh! I'm anxious. Don't talk."

A skinny guard in a green uniform and slightly tilted beret stood outside the orphanage entrance, motioning us in with one hand, a cigarette in the other. We funneled through a long, concrete corridor with bare walls. It smelled faintly of cigarette smoke, probably the guard's, and sweat, definitely ours. Why was I so anxious? I wasn't even there to adopt a child. When I grabbed my sister's hand she took it.

The corridor opened into a vast hall, teeming with hundreds of middle-aged Americans. The noise was deafening, trapped and amplified like an echo chamber. Group leaders screamed directions at their charges in English; orphanage employees, women wearing green sashes, like Girl Scouts, screamed at one another in Chinese; soon-to-be parents screamed questions at their group leaders, asking, *What is going on?* I wondered how a room packed with so many humans could be so cold.

Suddenly, a whistle cut through the noise, three bursts of Pay Attention! Pay Attention! Pay Attention! as dozens of nurses in white fitted uniforms and pointy white hats emerged into the chaos, each with an infant or toddler in her arms, speed-walking, fanning out in every direction. Watching them, it took a moment to understand their task: to match each baby with its rightful parents. Adoption group leaders were holding up signs, high above the crowd, to help direct them. The room got louder as the cries of petrified children mixed with the calls of the nurses.

"Hutch-in-son!"

"Mor-al-es!"

I felt as if I'd been plunged into the whirl of a hospital delivery room, where hundreds of women were simultaneously giving birth, assisted by humorless, unintelligible nurses.

Then suddenly, "Fel-cher!"

"Here! We're here!" my sister and I yelled, waving our arms.

"Your daughter, Yu Lin," the nurse said, foisting a swaddled, sleeping toddler into my arms.

"No! She's not mine! She's my sister's!" The nurse didn't hear me, or didn't care. With a swift pivot she was gone, pushing back through the crowd.

I handed Yu Lin to my sister, who planted a warm kiss on her daughter's cheek. Throughout the madness, Yu Lin slept, looking at peace. It was a good sign.

"Okay, mission accomplished. Let's get out of here," I said, craving the warmth of the van.

"Wait. Don't you want to kiss her?" my sister asked, holding Yu Lin out to me. Yes, I did, but not now. Now, I wanted to find the front entrance of that hall. Nevertheless, I bent down to give my niece a quick peck. As my lips touched her forehead, I felt a tug at my shoulder. It was the nurse.

"Wrong baby! Mistake! Wait here!" she commanded, and snatched the child away from us. Yu Lin was gone.

My sister and I stared at one another, speechless. What just happened? Standing there, I groped for words that would console her. *Don't worry, the next one will be just as good?* Before I could figure out what to say, the nurse was back again—with Yu Lin.

"No mistake! Yu Lin. She yours. Good luck!" she said, holding the still sleeping child out to me. My sister stepped forward for Yu Lin.

"Follow me," I ordered. "I don't want that woman to change her mind again."

That night in my sister's hotel room, after we'd given Yu Lin a bath and we put her down to sleep in the hotel crib, I confessed. I'd been devastated when the nurse had ripped Yu Lin away from us. I'd loved that child, no matter who she was. She was the baby I wanted, the baby our family deserved. Disarmed by the intensity of a feeling I had no name for, I asked my sister if she'd felt it too.

She knew exactly what it was.

"Of course," she told me. "You bonded. Like a mother."

And I thought, *Imagine that. I bonded with a baby*. In a million years, I could not have imagined a child could have made me feel like that.

Slipping into bed that night, exhausted, I was grateful for the solitude. Yet, I could not fall asleep. I thought of how peaceful Yu Lin looked amidst the tumult of that hall. I wondered how many babies had left the orphanage that day, in the arms of their new parents. I wondered how many Chinese girls were languishing in other orphanages. I tried to imagine what had gone through Yu Lin's mother's mind as she'd deposited her bundled-up daughter on the steps of a police station. I thought about my mailman Jimmy.

The next morning I knocked on my sister's door and offered to bring breakfast to her room. She had dark circles under her eyes. Yu Lin was napping—she'd been up most of the night.

"She wasn't really crying," my sister said. "It was more like a whimper. She probably thinks she's been kidnapped. Get me eggs and a lot of carbs."

When I got into the elevator on the eleventh floor it was empty. One floor down, a group of Chinese businessmen got on, all of them smoking, so I wedged myself into a back corner. Another floor down, two of the new mothers in our group got in, without their babies. They continued their conversation loudly, as if they were alone.

"Christmas is all I can think about. Before we left Minneapolis I bought her the most adorable little red velvet dress, with a big black velvet bow in the back. Finally, after all of these years I am going to have a baby on my lap for our family Christmas photo. This year the damn dog will be on the floor."

"For me, it's about Halloween. I've dreamed for so long about her costume. I can't wait to dress her up as a little princess or ballerina—or whatever she wants to be is okay with me. I just want to hold her tiny hand and take her out trick-or-treating. I can't wait to be a neighborhood mom!"

Listening to the mothers, I felt an overwhelming urge to push through the smoking businessmen, grab both women by their necks, and scream, *Is this your vision of parenthood—blissful holiday dress-up scenes? Boy, are you wrong, ladies! Over the next few years your adorable bundle of needs will cry inconsolably, have temper tantrums in public places, and projectile-vomit on your favorite dry-clean-only blouse. Before you know it, she'll be a teenager, smoking, drinking, taking drugs, and blaming everything she doesn't like about herself on you. I hope you've started a therapy fund!*

Where had that come from? Perhaps it was the fallout of too little sleep, or the accumulated stress of the trip. Scowling, I followed the Chinese businessmen and American mothers out of the elevator. Halfway across the lobby, making my way toward breakfast, I felt the muscles in my face relax, my jaw unclench, and my lips settle into a smirk, as I anticipated the story I'd tell Max, about how, the morning after we'd rescued Yu Lin, traveling from the ninth floor down to the first in the elevator of the Peace International Hotel in Nanchang, China, two loud, deliriously happy, clueless new mothers had reached deep into my soul and tapped the core of bona fide, immutable *me*.

Happily Ever After.

A recent *New Yorker* essay, "Imagining Ziggy," is the story of a couple choosing to become parents in their fifties, through IVF. It is at once a modern-day love story and an old-fashioned love song. "One of the reasons I began thinking about the actuality of having a child," Akhil

Sharma writes, "was that I was overflowing with love for my wife and wanted a place to put that love." The essay ends happily, with the birth of the couple's daughter, Ziggy.

Reading the essay, I was reminded of the Kissing Song:

(*Insert girl's name*) and (*Insert boy's name*),
Sitting in a tree,
K-I-S-S-I-N-G.
First comes love,
Then comes marriage,
Then comes baby,
In a baby carriage!

Though originally written as a lullaby, as kids we shouted the song from the top of our five-year-old lungs, to taunt any friend who dared show more attention to a boy than we considered appropriate. Lullaby or taunt, whispered or screamed, the rhyme endures as a road map, a directive sequence of events.

Love > Marriage > Baby.

Sharma superimposes his story onto this sequence in "Imagining Ziggy." He and his wife fall in love. They get married. They have a baby, a receptacle of their love, Ziggy.

Now, imagine a different ending. What if Sharma and his wife had been content to carry on into middle age without a child? What would their happy ending have been?

Love > Marriage > ?

This is my story. The story of a woman who fell in love with her quasi-professor and got married. The story of a woman who couldn't imagine a life more full. The story of a woman who never wanted a child. The story of a couple who never considered a child to be an appropriate receptacle for their love. The story of a couple who changed the default. The story of a woman with no regrets.

Confessions of a Skeleton Bride on Día de los Muertos

Stacey R. Forbes

November again and I stagger
like the walking dead to you:

the last lobo casting his eyes
on a ghost pepper moon.

The skin I shed for you
is not a costume—

though our consummation
is a strange parade.

You cup me like ceviche,
drum me like timbales,

make me a machete and I cull
from you the mariachi's holiest note.

I can still taste your tamarind mouth,
your whole corazón rimmed in salt.

A quickening of cicada wings
triggers my tongue—I sing too

of ruin and of resurrection.
Our timbre of hips is a tango,

a ripple in matchstick grass.
Mexican marigolds cling

to the earth for dear life on this day—
but the beauty of death is forever.

Roll the bones and tell me now,
how will we go—by water or by fire?

Love is the most natural disaster
of all. The small volcano

of your heart stirs in its sleep—
and I rise like the Sea of Cortez.

Yellow Footprints

Allison Fischer

A YOUNG WOMAN WITH SHOULDER-LENGTH, SAND-COLORED CURLS LAY entwined in her lover's arms, a thin top sheet the only thing covering their bare bodies. With her left pointer finger, she traced a faded black-and-white tattoo on her lover's forearm. The Greek letters spelled out the Latin phrase *semper fidelis,* which Dan had once told her meant "always faithful." Goosebumps erupted in the wake of her touch, and Dan shifted in his place behind her.

"What are you thinking about?"

He always knew when something was on her mind, and he never failed to ask after her thoughts. It was a stark contrast to her last lover, who had little care for her feelings, even when she was crying in front of him. The difference was jarring, and for a reason unknown to the young woman, she found it difficult to confide her true thoughts to Dan. It might have been the intimidating aura he gave off, or maybe it was their significant age difference that made her worry he would find her childish. Whatever the reason, Allison usually would end up telling him an edited version of her thoughts or blurting out something nonsensical and embarrassing.

"Nothing, really."

A blatant lie. Her head was so full of thoughts, she thought they might consume her. That wasn't new to Allison, and she had long convinced herself that Dan wouldn't want to be burdened with the truth of her storm-blown mind. Silence followed her lie. She ignored the little voice in the back of her mind that hoped Dan would press her for the truth. He didn't. As he settled against her back and drifted off, she shoved down her disappointment, in both him and herself. Instead, she lay awake, and let herself spiral into her ever present anxieties.

The present semester had started a few months ago. Desperate to meet her family's expectations (namely, her mother's), she had changed her major for the third time, hoping this one might inspire her to stick with classes. It hadn't. With half the semester left to go, she was already failing three out of her four classes. No matter what she did, Allison couldn't bring herself to attend classes past the first few weeks. They bored her, and the pile of homework was so overwhelming, it made a terrible feeling she couldn't name claw at her throat. She had struggled with school since sixth grade, failing enough classes to require summer school twice. With each failure, her confidence dropped until she became convinced she was just stupid. Her parents thought she was lazy. They became increasingly furious with what they considered her lackluster effort until one day, they blew up. Her father later said it was supposed to motivate her to pass. She'd made it through high school by the skin of her teeth. Now in college, his words had haunted her along with every failure.

If you don't pass your classes and at least get your diploma, you'll end up with no way to support yourself except as a prostitute! Is that what you want?

Almost four years later, when others from her class were just a few months away from earning their degrees, Allison had a grand total of nine credits and a score of incompletes. It made her want to scream and toss all her books out of her car window, but she was desperate not to disappoint her parents. So, she kept going, finding the time for classes in between her forty-, sometimes fifty-hour work weeks at Turkey Hill.

The convenience store had been a much-needed escape from her tumultuous home life for the last three years. She worked hard and took on as many extra shifts as she could, so that she wouldn't have to go home until her family was asleep. Since she started getting serious with Dan, she spent most evenings in his bed, only going home to wash clothes. Unfortunately, she had secured a job for her ex-boyfriend at Turkey Hill after they had broken up. From a place of refuge, her job became another source of stress.

With a sigh, Allison forced her thoughts away from the man who had caused her nothing but pain and turned her thoughts to the one pressed against her back. She looked down at the arm wrapped around her waist, eyes tracing over the tattoo again. The words were Dan's tribute to his years in the Marine Corps. The way he reminisced with fondness about his former comrades, deployments, and the ridiculous and often dangerous shenanigans he got into as a young Marine sent an unfamiliar shiver of excitement through her. He had done and seen so much. Was that the reason for his quiet confidence and intimidating air? Would she be able to do amazing things? Could she also learn to feel comfortable in her own skin?

Then, the image of her mother's face, drawn, with once bright blue eyes listless and her lips stuck in a permanent reflection of her grief, rose in her head to combat the hopeful thoughts. At the tender age of three, Allison had watched as the paramedics rushed Mommy to the ER to stitch up the bloody, too-deep lines carved down the length of both her arms. Her father dropped her off at the babysitter with little word of comfort or explanation of what was happening. Several other children played on the wooden play set in the backyard without a care in the world. She sat alone on the top deck of the pretend pirate ship, waiting with dread for Daddy to come back and tell her that Mommy was gone. She didn't cry. Couldn't. There was a strange hollowness in her chest that she'd never felt before, blocking the tears from coming. While the other children ran about the yard, fighting imaginary enemies with play swords, little Allison wondered what she had done to make her mother so sad that she hurt herself. All she had wanted was for Mommy to unlock the door and play with her. That day, she promised to be a better daughter, to make her mom happy so she would never have to hurt herself again. Since then, she'd done whatever she could to keep Kelly from slipping back into that darkest of places, even if that meant keeping her own feelings locked away.

HOW COULD ALLISON EVEN think of leaving? How could she be that selfish? And who would take care of Mom if she left? Her brothers and father weren't up to the task, and Angie, her mom's new girlfriend, was too new to the family to be burdened with it. No. Joining the military was nothing but a selfish, fleeting thought that needed to be buried and forgotten.

For months, Allison thought of nothing but school, work, and her mom. Her relationship with Dan didn't last long, giving her another reason to put the Marines out of her mind. No matter how hard she tried, however, the idea pricked at the back of her mind again and again. Like the needles of a tattoo gun carving a picture into her skin, the image of herself in that tan camo uniform, hair pulled tight into a sleek bun, and sleeves rolled and pressed with a perfect edge, was inked into her skull.

She distracted herself with another lover, a man twice her age with four fire-haired children. He showered her with compliments, always reminding her of how beautiful or smart he thought she was. She almost believed it, wanted him to be right more than anything. He made her feel wanted. She adored the two youngest children, and the relationship between Chris and his teenage daughter had eerie parallels to her own relationship with her parents. The girl, who was only a few years younger than her, went back and forth between keeping her feelings locked away, to lashing out at her dad, whom she blamed for their mother leaving. Chris responded in kind by coming down hard on his oldest child, treating the smallest of mistakes like they would ruin the girl's entire future. If Chris had some perspective from someone closer to his daughter's age, maybe she could help their relationship heal. It was selfish of Allison to dream of leaving everything behind when there were so many people she could help here.

But the dream persisted until the almost twenty-two-year-old couldn't ignore it any longer.

She had been sitting in the school cafeteria one morning with her laptop when it finally happened. She was supposed to be in sociology (a class she detested almost as much as its teacher), but Allison was instead reading through every page of the Marines website: from the history of the corps to what boot camp would be like, to the hundreds of different jobs she could have. Once she navigated back to the home page, the stark white bold letters that read "Request Information" were impossible to ignore. She gave in. It wouldn't hurt anyone just to learn more, right? If she talked to someone at the recruitment office, she could get the ridiculous idea out of her head. She would realize that military life wasn't for her and go on with her day.

Of course, that wasn't how it went at all.

A recruiter at the local office reached out to her within twenty-four hours. The next week, Allison sat in front of his desk, sorting a dozen little black rectangular tiles with words etched in white ink, arranging them from most important to least. Self-Confidence, Self-Discipline, and Self-Reliance found their way into the top three with little thought. Her manager at Turkey Hill, Ryan, had warned her that recruiters would spew whatever lies they could to convince Allison to sign her life away. She believed him. The Marine Corps was the smallest branch of the military, with the highest quotas and which met the most resistance from worried parents. Of course, recruiters would have to get creative.

Sergeant Wical was a handsome, charismatic man with a laugh that made you feel at ease. Experience taught her that men like that could lie with a grin on their face and think nothing of it, but she didn't need any pretty words or false promises from him. She had made her decision the moment her fingers brushed over the hopeful words etched into the cold ceramic tiles. What Allison wanted more than anything, in that insignificant moment in time, was to join the ranks of the few proud men and women who worked hard to earn the title of

United States Marine. For the first time since she was a little girl who only knew how to want, Allison made a conscious choice, one that she knew might hurt people she loved, but that was wholly for herself.

That decision was the hardest of any to stand by. Almost as if the universe was challenging her resolve, it threw everything it could at her in the next few months to make the young woman change her mind. The most difficult was the revelation that her grandmother was suffering from late-stage throat cancer. Allison put her commitment to the Marines on hold as she traveled with Angie and her mother to visit her Grandma Grant, who they fondly called GG, in the nursing home. She sat at GG's bedside, trying not to choke on the smell of bleach, which failed to mask the noxious scent of vomit and urine. Her grandmother, who she remembered always having a bright grin on her face, turned to Allison with a pained grimace as she asked, "How are you doing in school?"

Allison had bitten her lip, hesitant, but mustered up the courage to answer. "I dropped out of college. I'm going to join the Marines."

She had expected admonishment. Their family saw success as earning a degree and making good money. The military wasn't an option. Instead of scolding, or asking why, GG only cried. Allison watched the silent tears find their way through the deep lines of GG's face, dripping from her chin to the scratchy tan hospital blanket covering her lap with shock and a heap of shame. Never, in her almost twenty-two years of life, had she witnessed her GG cry.

Not when her grandkids knocked into one of her pain-ridden, sarcoid-covered legs.

Nor when Grandpa Gary disowned her mom for being married to a woman, and GG had watched from inside the car as Kelly and her grandkids got smaller and smaller as they drove away from the hotel they had met at.

Not even when Allison had lost her temper after being scolded for talking to her little cousin about her two mothers, screaming at GG that she was an awful person for shunning her daughter.

For her to make the older woman cry, she must have done something terrible. Guilt stuck in her throat, making it hard to breathe, and Allison rose from the chair and ran from the room before her mother or Angie could say a word.

For a few months after returning home, Allison avoided Sergeant Wical at all costs. All his calls went to voicemail. Emails and text messages went unread. They had made nothing official, so she had no obligation other than good manners to answer him, and the shame was still too fresh. What could she say to him? What excuse could she offer, other than she made her dying grandmother cry, that would justify her sudden choice to back out? He was practically a stranger. She wasn't about to tell him her sob story. He would give up in no time. There were plenty of other people desperate to get out of their dying, crime infested city.

She went back to school after a fourth (and final, she promised herself) change of major, determined to succeed this time. Everything was going right for once. Her high school boyfriend quit his job at Turkey Hill, so she didn't have to deal with him. She and her new boyfriend, Chris, were spending more and more time together. Her mom and Angie were talking about marriage.

Then she came home from work late one evening to her mother's wrenching sobs, echoing down the stairwell through her closed bedroom door. GG was gone. She had chosen, against everyone's pleas, to stop treatment and live out the rest of her days in the home she had built her life in.

At the service, everyone spoke of how generous she was, how she lived her life for others and in service to God. GG was the glue that held their family together, Aunt Patty said. The programs featured black-and-white pictures of one of her grandmother's paintings, and they had decorated the funeral home with them.

While her children, sisters, and husband spoke of her generosity, sacrifice, and incredible strength, Allison couldn't help but wonder what might have happened if GG hadn't given up her career as a nurse to raise four children, or if she had dedicated more time to her beautiful paintings. Would Allison have been able to view one of her precious works of art in a museum? Or maybe she could have become the breadwinner for the family, with a long and fulfilling career at the local hospital. Allison would never know, because GG had put everyone before herself until her last days. It wasn't the wrong choice, but Allison at last understood it was the wrong choice for her. She didn't want to spend the rest of her life doing what would make everyone else happy, even if she hated it.

Just days after the funeral, Allison walked into Sergeant Wical's office and apologized for blowing him off. She told him everything, about her grandmother's cancer and death, about her fear of disappointing her mother, or worse, not being there to pull her back from the edge. The young woman held her head high, wiping the tears from her eyes with the back of her sleeve, and met the recruiter's stare as she said, "There's nothing holding me back now. I'm ready. How soon can you get me sworn in?"

Sergeant Wical held her stare, looking for any sign of hesitation. When he found none, the amiable smile returned to his face as he answered.

"We can go through the paperwork today and get a drug test done. If that comes back negative, we can ship you up to MEPS to swear in next week. As long as you make it through the screening process up there, we'll be able to give you a date for when you'll be leaving for boot camp. Once you swear in, there's no backing out. Are you sure you're ready?"

"Yes."

There was nothing but conviction in her answer. The following week, she rode for three intense hours to the processing station in Harrisburg with Sergeant Wical and two other soon-to-be recruits. He escorted them into the building and signed them in. He then turned to them, smile gone from his lips in favor of a stern expression as he gave them a last reminder.

"The job of everyone in this building is to weed out those who aren't fit to serve. Don't give them a reason to declare you unfit because it's difficult to appeal. Whatever it says on your paperwork, those are the answers you give to questions. If they catch you lying, you will be permanently barred from military service. They will put you under immense stress to get you to confess to anything you might be hiding, even threaten you with jail time. Don't let it scare you. When you're done, I'll meet you in the oath office."

The next few hours felt like a lifetime. They had arrived in Harrisburg just an hour after sunrise. By the time she made it through the grueling questions and terrifying threats and rejoined Sergeant Wical in the oath office, the sun had almost set. Allison knew she would fall asleep the moment her head hit the cold glass of the car window. The group was instructed to form four lines, facing an American flag hanging off one wall. A thrill swept through her veins, fighting off the settling weariness. Sergeant Wical stood at the front of the room, along with a handful of other recruiters, dressed in the signature pressed khaki blouse and royal blue trousers with the red blood stripe sewn along the length of the leg. The white vinyl caps with shining black brims were tucked under their arms.

Next to them, the oath officer explained the oath they were about to take, making them practice the words until every soon-to-be recruit could repeat the oath without stumbling. The officer called them to attention, and Allison snapped her eyes forward, arms tight against her sides with hands balled into fists, and brought her feet together, heels touching and toes pointed out in a V. Sergeant Wical had stressed before they left that morning when he taught them how to come into the position, not to lock out their knees. He would never let them live it down if any of them passed out. Allison took the advice to heart, keeping a slight bend in her knees as the oath officer instructed them to repeat after him, though with the way her heart was hammering against her chest, she might pass out anyway. Unable to shake her head to relieve the stress,

Allison took a deep breath instead as she said her oath of enlistment.

"I, Allison Simmons, do solemnly swear that I will support and defend the Constitution of the United States against all enemies, foreign and domestic; that I will bear true faith and allegiance to the same; and that I will obey the orders of the President of the United States and the orders of the officers appointed over me, according to regulations and the Uniform Code of Military Justice. So help me God."

It was done. The oath officer dismissed the group into the care of their respective recruiters, and Sergeant Wical let the amiable smile spread across his face as she and the two boys she came with approached him. He shook each of their hands and said, "Congratulations, you are now official recruits of the United States Marine Corps. I'm proud to serve with you."

Her chest swelled, and joyful tears sprung in her eyes.

The month and a half before her ship date passed in the blink of an eye. Sergeant Wical and the other recruiters had kept her busy with grueling physical training. They ran miles through the forest in a line on Saturdays, passing a weighted baton back until it reached the last person, who then had to sprint to the front while trying not to trip over loose rocks or tree roots on the trail. She, who had always preferred music and sitting in a comfortable corner with a book to things like sports, struggled to meet Sergeant Wical's high expectations, but she pushed through, determined to head to boot camp with the best possible advantage she could manage.

And so, here she was almost two months later, likely just minutes away from the goal she had longed for. Silvery rays from the moon filtered in through the bus windows as it made its way southeast, leaving the small town on the border of Georgia where her plane had landed, and across the wide expanse of South Carolina to the tiny island that would be her home for the next few months. The giant steel box and its driver were undeterred by the unlit, empty road, but a heavy, apprehensive silence oppressed its passengers. Around forty young men and women sat in pairs on the weathered leather seats. There was no way for the group to know their location, and yet they all seemed to sense that their destination was drawing near.

The group had filled the start of the ride with chatter. The recruits swapped stories of their childhood homes, their aspirations for the future within the military, and their reasons for joining. Each recruit had a vastly different background and motive, and Allison wondered how the drill instructors would transform this wild, diverse gang, all just barely adults, into uniformed soldiers who obeyed orders without question. Now that the conversation had died down, the young recruits stared out the window or into their laps with anxious faces. They looked even younger somehow, even less like future Marines.

She remembered the conversation she had with her recruiter just before he dropped her off at the hotel in Harrisburg. He said that every recruit had a moment where they asked themselves what the hell they were doing there. Why had they signed up for this hell? His own, like many, was the moment their own bus of recruits arrived at the recruit depot on Parris Island. The moment when the first of their many drill instructors, with their cold eyes under their signature olive green campaign covers with the extra wide brim, had stepped into the bus and screamed so loud that it echoed off the aluminum walls and nearly deafened him.

When would her moment come?

The bus slowed, then came to a stop. She peered out the window, trying to glimpse the island, but it was too dark. The doors opened with a hiss, and a dark-skinned mountain of a man with arms as large as tree trunks, wide-brimmed hat tipped low over his fierce eyes, stepped into the aisle and said with a booming rasp that rattled her bones, "What the hell are you looking at, piss ants? Put your goddamn heads down against the seats and listen!"

Everyone rushed to comply. Allison peeked at the terrified faces of her comrades from behind the leather seat back. There was no doubt. At least half of them were regretting their decision, a few even had tears welling in their eyes. Her heart was hammering against her chest again, but not with anxiety or dread. Excitement thrummed in her veins as she listened to the burly drill instructor scream instructions.

"You will exit in a single-file line and make your way to my yellow footprints! You will keep your heads forward and your mouths shut. Do not move off those footprints until I tell you! If you take even a step off my footprints or whisper a word, you will regret the day you were born! If one of my drill instructors addresses you, you will call them Sir or Ma'am! When you answer a question, you will scream like your life depends on it! Is that understood? Scream 'Aye-Aye, Sir!'"

"Aye-Aye, Sir!" the recruits answered.

The drill instructor's face screwed up in fury, and spittle flew from his mouth as he yelled, "Louder!"

"AYE-AYE, SIR!" Some of the recruits' voices cracked as they struggled to answer.

"Now get the hell out of this bus and onto those yellow footprints! Scream 'Aye-Aye, Sir!'"

"AYE-AYE, SIR!"

Everyone scrambled to follow his orders, grabbing what little belongings they brought and rushing out of the bus. Allison shimmied into the aisle. On her recruiter's advice, she had chosen not to bring anything with her. It would only be taken and shoved into a brown paper bag with her name scribbled on it in black sharpie until she graduated. Even her phone was left with her mom. They would bring it to her when they picked her up on graduation day.

She kept her head forward as she followed the line, not daring to let her curiosity get the best of her as she stepped onto a small set of sun-colored footsteps painted onto the black tar. The girl in front of her shook like a leaf as several more wide-brimmed hats swarmed around them, their screaming blending together and the words difficult to pick apart. Her arms and legs trembled as well, but Allison suspected it wasn't for the same reason. It was all she could do to keep the grin off her face.

At last, after a year of doubt and struggle, she was here. The months ahead would be the most challenging of her life, but they were hers. Allison had made this choice for no one but herself, and the power that instilled in her drowned out any fear. She would hold that eagle, globe, and anchor in her hand and transform into a woman with strength and surety.

The drill instructors of November Company worked hard to drive the moment of regret into her. The next forty-eight hours were filled with screaming, confusion, and zero sleep as they processed the newest batch of recruits. A pile of gear that she had no clue how to use was thrust into arms that had gone numb from the series of vaccinations needed to prevent illnesses that she'd never heard of. A giant rucksack was filled to the brim with uniforms, a bulky vest filled with ceramic bulletproof plates, magazine and grenade pouches, a gas mask, and a dozen other items, which made the sack so heavy, she struggled to lift it onto her back. Coupled with her exhaustion, the hike back from the supply issue left her legs shaking. Once she was finally permitted to sleep, Allison collapsed onto the hard mattress of her bunk bed, one of twenty arranged in two parallel lines along the concrete walls of her squad bay. She could have slept for days, but four hours was all the time allotted to her before being ripped from a dreamless sleep to start the day's training. The glimpse of sky from the barred windows was still pitch black. It would be another two hours before the sun rose, but that didn't stop them from being herded into the chow hall to scarf down as much as they could in fifteen minutes before being led out to the grassy training grounds. In the dark, the multitude of fire-ant hills that dotted the grass were impossible to spot, and more than one recruit jumped up from their morning stretches with surprised shrieks of pain, only to be rounded on by their unsympathetic drill instructors for interrupting.

By week four, the comfortable layer of fat on her body, formed by years of a sedentary lifestyle and lazy diet, was gone, replaced by lithe muscles in her arms, legs, and core. Even her face had thinned, high cheekbones more pronounced than ever. Her friends back home would be concerned by the rapid transformation, but Allison had never felt stronger. She no longer wheezed and lagged behind during runs, and the weight of her pack, which she had buckled under at the start, was little more than a school bag. She could throw one of her fellow recruits over her shoulder and run with them or hold them in place as she squatted during their morning exercises. The first phase of boot camp, designed to tear them down to nothing, had come to a close. Week five marked the beginning of the second phase, the build-up, where they would learn the skills shared by all Marines. Allison had been looking forward to combat training more than anything else, and so couldn't contain her excitement the morning they were led to the dirt pits for their first instruction.

The martial arts instructor's firm but uplifting lessons were a welcome break from the constant belittling of their usual wardens. They were still Marines, but the black T-shirts in place of a pressed blouse and crisply rolled sleeves and the lack of wide-brimmed hats covering steel eyes put them at ease. Allison listened intently, eyes never straying from the woman at the front of the group as she demonstrated a chokehold. They were then divided into pairs to practice. A tawny-haired girl whose name she couldn't remember approached her with a relaxed grin, something that would have earned her a trip to the sand pit and a hundred push-ups if their drill instructors caught sight of it. She settled into a fighting stance, fists held too low to block a hit in time, and feet too close together as she said, "I'll go first. Just tap out so the instructors think we're doing it right. Then we can switch, and I'll do the same thing."

Allison raised a brow but said nothing, moving into her own stance, fists held on either side of her face and feet shoulder-width apart. She crouched low, keeping her center of gravity close to the ground so she would be harder to push off balance. Her partner snapped forward, grabbing onto one arm to twist it behind her back while sweeping her feet out from under her. She hit the dirt, her partner's arm locked around her throat, but there was no pressure applied to her airway. The other recruit held her, waiting for Allison to tap out so they could switch, but she refused, and one of the instructors took notice and approached. She looked down at them with a scowl and said, "Let her go and both of you get up."

"Aye-Aye, Ma'am!"

They hurried to stand and come to attention. The instructor turned to Allison and asked, "Why didn't you tap out?"

"Ma'am! This recruit didn't tap out because she wasn't choking me, Ma'am!"

From the side, where the instructor couldn't see, her partner shot her a sour look, but Allison ignored it. She wasn't here to goof off or make friends, and fudging the training would only come back to bite her at the end when she couldn't pass the assessment. The instructor hid a snort of laughter by ducking her chin for a moment, a common tactic used when one of the recruits did something funny and they didn't want to lose their bearing, though the lack of a campaign cover to hide her expression made it less effective. When she looked back up, her face was blank again as she said, "Switch and show her how to do it right, then."

"Aye-Aye, Ma'am!" Allison answered and turned back to her partner, who was flushed pink with anger and embarrassment. She tried not to feel too guilty as she shifted back into a fighting stance. It hadn't been her intention to get the girl in trouble. The instructor took a moment to correct her partner's stance before telling them to go. She surged forward, copying the grab and twist and locking her elbow around the girl's throat as she pushed her chest into the dirt, using her right hand to grab her left fist and tighten the hold until a satisfying choking sound was dragged from the girl's lips. She reveled in the feeling of her partner's stubborn struggling underneath her. The moment her partner's hand slapped the dirt, she let go and backed away, looking at the instructor for approval. She nodded with the ghost of a smirk on her face and said, "Good. Hart, you will practice with me. Simmons, you can work on your punches and kicks until we move on."

The boost of confidence from the rare moment of praise energized her throughout the rest of the day. Even when she messed up during drill and her primary drill instructor, known as the kill hat, pulled her out of the formation, ordering her to hold her rifle out in front of her until it felt like her arms were about to fall off, her mood didn't dim.

At week five, as they stood outside the chow hall waiting for their turn to eat, their senior drill instructor, referred to as Senior, caught Ramirez, their platoon leader, laughing as she conversed with the squad leaders. She was the second guide to be unceremoniously fired that week. The first time, Senior had chosen Ramirez from among the squad leaders to be the replacement. This time, she stood at the front of the chow hall as the recruits finished eating and asked for volunteers. For a few minutes, no one spoke. Then Henderson, their original guide, rose from her seat, only to be shot down before she had a chance to speak. Allison looked around the room at her comrades, waiting for one of them to step up. When no one did, she scarfed down the last bite of her bland lunch and stood, arms clamped tight to her sides as she said as loud as she could, "Ma'am! This recruit volunteers for the position, Ma'am!"

Senior, a beautiful woman with smooth skin and dark eyes that were kinder than anyone's she'd ever met, stared her down. She raised a brow as she took in Allison's earnest but unkempt appearance. Her wild curls had proved impossible to tame, and Senior had threatened to make her cut it on multiple occasions. Unlike some of the other girls, she had no military experience, and struggled to force her hair into the signature slick donut-shaped bun. Stray curls stuck out at all angles, and by the end of the day, her bun had often come undone entirely. Senior pursed her lips, waiting another moment for anyone else to volunteer, before she gave in and said, "Since you're the only one who managed to stand up and address me properly, you've got it. But your hair had better be perfect tomorrow morning."

"Aye-Aye, Ma'am!"

She'd never struggled so hard not to smile in her life. One of the squad leaders was kind enough to gel and braid her hair for her that night after lights out, so that come morning it was flawless.

Weeks six and seven were range week. Allison had never imagined she would feel so comfortable with a rifle tucked into her shoulder. The only experience she had with a gun was the one time at summer camp when they'd gone to the range and shot fake deer with a shotgun. She had been a terrible shot, not even grazing the target once. But as she lay in the grass, elbows kept tight to her body for the best support, and practiced her slow, controlled breathing as she took aim at a rusted steel barrel with several bright yellow targets painted on it through her scope, she was at ease and brimming with confidence. Her kill hat came up behind her. She tensed, waiting for the usual derision that accompanied her presence. The woman never had a kind word for her, not that she expected any. It came as a surprise then, when she only smirked down at her and said before moving on, "I think Simmons wants to shoot. Maybe you'll finally be good at something other than hiking."

She almost slipped up and let her shock show on her face. That was two compliments in one sentence. Invigorated, she returned her eye to the scope, making sure to keep the other eye open as she breathed deep. She compressed the trigger with a slow, controlled pull as she exhaled. The empty rifle clicked, but she imagined a hole appearing dead center of the target in her sights. She checked to make sure no one was watching before allowing a wide grin to spread across her face for a moment, wiping it away as soon as her kill hat came back into view.

AT LAST, AFTER THREE of the most difficult months of her life, the second to last week of boot camp was ending as Allison led her platoon on the hike home, having completed their three-day-long graduation assessment, the Crucible, and earned the right to call herself a Marine. She wasn't a guide or squad leader anymore. Her leadership position had only lasted about a week, but that was par for the course, and she didn't let it bother her. Despite not being a platoon leader, Senior had pulled her to the front of the formation because she was the best hiker in the platoon. She needed people who could keep the proper pace at the front for their return from the Crucible, which would be witnessed by nearly everyone on the island. Allison held her head high, no longer needing to hide her grin as she marched. Her tan camouflage utility uniform, with the painstakingly starched and ironed rolled sleeves, was covered in dirt, and she, like the rest of her platoon, stank of sweat. The smell had sunk so deep into her blouse and trousers and the dirt was so thick, she would have to soak the uniform in a tub of bleach to get the filth out. Her feet ached, and the soles of her boots were so worn she could feel every slap of her toes against the pavement. Still, as the sun rose behind them, bathing the platoon with its summer warmth, and they rounded the corner onto the main street that led through Parris Island, she joined her drill instructors and new comrades in their uplifting cadence, screaming "MARINE CORPS" after each line Senior sang.

> *A 1, 2, 3, 4*
> *A 1, 2, 3, 4*
> *A ARMY, NAVY WAS NOT FOR ME*
> *AIR FORCE WAS JUST A TOO EASY*
> *WHAT I NEED WAS A LITTLE BIT MORE*
> *I NEED A LIFE THAT IS HARDCORE*
> *PARRIS ISLAND IS WHERE IT BEGAN*
> *A LITTLE ROCK WITH LOTSA SAND*
> *I CAN'T FORGET ABOUT HOLLYWOOD*
> *SAN DIEGO AND IT'S ALL GOOD*
> *PT DRILL ALL DAY LONG*
> *KEEP ME RUNNING FROM DUSK TO DAWN*

A 1, 2, 3, 4
TELL ME NOW WHAT YOU WAITING FOR
A 1, 2, 3, 4
MOMMA NOW I'M GONNA SING YOU SOME MORE
FIRST PHASE IT BROKE ME DOWN
SECOND PHASE I STARTED COMIN' ROUND
THIRD PHASE I WAS LEAN AND MEAN
GRADUATION STANDING TALL IN MY GREEN
TO ANYBODY WHO ASKED ME WHY
HERE'S THE DEAL I GAVE MY REPLY
I'LL BE A MARINE TIL THE DAY I DIE
MOTIVATED AND SEMPER FI

Her drill instructors timed the end of the cadence perfectly with the end of their hike as they came to a stop in front of the Iwo Jima Memorial. They scrambled to drop their packs and arrange them in four neat rows, before forming ranks five steps away from the stone statue. Senior took post at the head of the formation and called them to attention so she could give instructions.

"When I step in front of you, you will go to rest, receive your eagle, globe, and anchor with your left hand, and go back to attention when I move to the next person."

Her heart pounded as Senior made her rounds. What felt like an hour before the drill instructor stepped in front of her was really only half that, but her sore feet and sleep deprivation made the wait agonizing. At last, Senior arrived, and she addressed the drill instructor by her rank, a privilege earned along with her new title.

"Good morning, Staff Sergeant."

She held her hand out, heart stuttering as the black eagle, globe, and anchor, no bigger than a quarter, was placed in her sweating, open palm. Staff Sergeant offered her a secret smile as she said under her breath, "Good morning, Marine. Congratulations. You earned this."

She stepped away. Allison snapped back to attention, clutching the little pin that she had worked so hard for in her hand. She kept the silent, joyful tears at bay until her drill instructor made it to the end of her row. A subtle glance on either side revealed that most of her comrades were crying as well. Their official graduation ceremony would take place in a few days, with just enough time to celebrate Independence Day with their family as new Marines. Her parents would get to see the results of all her efforts, and Allison was proud to show them. She couldn't wait to stand in front of them in her dress uniform, trousers pressed with fresh, perfect creases, shoes shined, and hair pulled back tight and sleek. Allison imagined their awe as they watched her march onto the stage, rifle held tight against her shoulder as she moved with her platoon in sharp, synchronized movement. For the first time in years, she was confident in the future ahead, so she took a moment to appreciate the men and women who came before her. Thanks to them, Allison would build a life that she could enjoy and be proud of. She would sacrifice her life if she was called to, but she would never again sacrifice her wellness for the sake of someone else's happiness. The bright yellow footsteps she had stood on three months ago were the start of a meaningful, fulfilling future, and nothing and no one would take it away from her. From that moment on, the words inked into Dan's arm, *always faithful*, would hold new meaning. Allison would strive to remain always faithful to her own heart.

Tattoo Poem

Maria Nazos

Sometimes, to truly appreciate the fact
that you're still alive, you must wake up
pressed next to a sweaty, snoring heap
of a man who hours ago declared his love

for you, armed robbery, and murder, in that
order. And you think of how, of all the places
between degrees in your life you could have
ended up, this one really isn't so bad—

You'd always envisioned a post-breakup
breakdown as quieter, less erotic, but here
you go, here you are—piles of filthy laundry
and medieval-looking needles and tribal

designs on the walls. No, you didn't get
a tattoo, not this time. But every poem
about failure should have at least one:
you've inked your sorrow on yourself

in places you can't even see, and if someone
were just to look at you, they'd never know
how many times you've floundered, never due
to any glamorous misstep, but usually because

you had trouble hiding your mess—But now,
you can't anymore, and there's beauty in that,
too. It's here, next to you, sticky as rock
candy, pure as uncut coke. Earlier, you patiently

explained to the man that given his lengthy criminal
record, the fact you're dirt-poor and still in school,
and that he's probably a dangerous human being,
that marriage is currently out of the cards.

He smiled, shy as a girl, proud that you figured
out at least part of him without losing sight
of the details—that he's still a kind man, one
who earlier nursed you back to health with ramen:

you shook in his inking chair from too much blow.
Now, touch his damp, scarred cheek. Whether it's love
you're still breathing, or that life is crawling with mostly
good people, even if they are the occasional semi-

reformed serial killer, you're happy to be here. So, before
you slip out the back door, step behind the curtain
that serves as a bathroom. Under the low hanging
light bulb, try your best to imagine a wedge of sun

beneath your eyes. Then rub away your bleary vision
and walk out, hung-over into the harsh, bright
afternoon—No, you don't get to leave this world
without carrying the mark of something.

Visiting the Queen

Barbara Tylla

The old queen sits on a bench in Bryant Park.
She sits as always stiff backed and regal
her tote bags sprawled beside her on the bench.
She comes to the park to feed the pigeons.
I come to the park to visit the queen.

She hasn't shaved today and perhaps
that is the reason for the hostile stares.
They do not see the royalty
behind the purple dress,
the grandeur in the ballet slippers.
They see only an old queen;
a rouged and powdered relic
that no one needs or treasures, anymore.

She isn't bothered by the stares,
and I am awed by her courage.
I am not brave enough
to take my shoes off in the park.
I would not have the courage to endure
the hostile stares.

She goes about her business
with quiet resolution.
First, she scatters popcorn for the pigeons
who bow and coo at her feet like tiny
feathered suitors begging her for royal favors.
Then from a giant tote bag
she takes out a bowl of pineapple,
which she begins to eat with relish
with the aid of a plastic fork.

She nods to me and holds up a slice of fruit,
but I shake my head and rush to the safety of my book.
My heart is pounding. Has she seen beneath
my knotted tie? Does she recognize the princess
trapped inside the suited man?

I do not know the answers to these questions
but perhaps it doesn't matter
because the queen has crossed the walk
to my park bench and handed me
the bowl of pineapple.
Her voice is gentle. "Take one," she says,
and holds out a second fork.

And so, we sit in Bryant Park
the old queen and the even older princess.
We eat pineapple slices with plastic forks
and watch the pigeons
puff and swagger at our feet.
What will happen when the pineapple is finished?
Perhaps, nothing.

Perhaps, I will just take off my shoes.

Elsewhere

A.L. Rowser

WHAT'S SCARIER THAN A HORSE? ERICA DELATORRE WOULD PROMPT HER KIDS. *A bampire horse!* Dylan would scream-laugh while Penny made this vampire-horse face with teeth clenched and lips drawn back to show off her missing front tooth. Erica had been percolating this idea for a children's book, or maybe YA, but when she'd shared it with Joel, he just rolled his eyes. *Well, that's stupid. You've seen horse teeth, right?* And somehow, she'd let his reaction slide. Even that, she'd let slide. But this was before California's COVID-19 lockdown.

And now, here they were, three weeks deep into a routine so precariously balanced that Erica didn't know how much longer she could keep it up. It was 10 a.m. on a Wednesday, and she had just pressed record on her scheduled client call, when Joel burst out of the bedroom-turned-office with their son, leaving the door wide open to the cacophony of Penny and her fellow second graders' morning recitation. This week it was the long "o." Something with a ghost (which seemed advanced given the silent "h") that involved sewing, maybe snow and a toad?

Joel left the door to the bathroom open as well so she was privy (ha ha) to all the potty prep. (Funny not funny, right?) Something seriously had to give.

Erica had taken up ghostwriting when Dylan, their youngest, started preschool last year. The company she worked for, Author-ize Yourself, Inc., promoted a cookie-cutter book-writing approach for businesspeople eager to establish authority in their niche. While it sounded simple enough—recording to transcript to significantly cleaned up chapters—clients needed significant handholding on the planning and recording part. And now, with her family home, she lacked the necessary presence of mind to even guide herself.

Erica swallowed her irritation and muted her microphone—relieved only that there was no camera involved to take in the mounds of background clutter or her stained T-shirt and hair slicked up in a bun-meets-ponytail, the bags under her eyes and the bad skin that seemed outright unfair at thirty-seven.

"Big boys make big poop!" Dylan boasted from the bathroom.

"Just keep goin', buddy."

You have the whole house! Joel accused, when she complained about these disruptions. *I hardly have it*, she'd throw back at him, *when you're waltzing around, even talking to me, while I'm on a call! I can't just put the phone down until they're done like you do with your mother. I have to give feedback, ask questions.* She shouldn't have brought his mother into it, but it was difficult to keep arguments above the belt when the other person refused.

Erica stared at the black material of a shirt slung over the back of a dining room chair in front of her and imagined everything else similarly blacked out—everything but the voice of Hilda Donaldson, promoting her business under the guise of a how-to book. "Chapter two will focus on workflow," Hilda stated. "You'll notice 'workflow' is one word. This is because the flow is just as important as the work. Without 'flow,' the word itself remains incomplete, as well as the work, which at the very least—"

Clapping crescendoed over the whoosh of flushing. As Erica's outrage surged, a ripple moved through the fabric of the shirt. There were no stripes, no design that might cause an optical illusion. Yet, there it was. Erica closed her eyes, took a calming breath. Her son just needed to use the bathroom. What else was Joel supposed to do? *Close the damn door.* For starters.

"In this chapter, you're going to go from overwhelmed to confident with peace of mind," Hilda Donaldson stated. "I will now lay out all the steps for you to get started." Her voice was similar to the one Erica used when reading a story to put the kids to sleep, monotonous enough that try as she might to imagine the parade of words across a page, the "steps" appeared as jumbles of unidentifiable pieces coming down an assembly line.

But Hilda must have a chapter outline. All clients completed that step before coming to Erica. In her distracted state, she had simply forgotten to pull it up. "Workflow" she typed into the search window. She opened the only document to appear.

"No one likes a nag," Pearl's mother would chastise her.

Yet why be a likeable maid when you could be anything else? As Pearl did her algebra homework, she thought of her future potential not as a fixed "x" or "y" to solve for. Instead, it should shift and change, resisting a value that could be pinned down. So, she represented her future aspirations in this way, with a space.

"Well, I don't assume people will like . . . either."

These spaces functioned like potholes, visibly tripping her mother up. As hard as she tried to blink them away, to step over or past them, every time Pearl set one out, her mother dropped something or fumbled.

In the time it had taken Erica to muddle through what was clearly some story remnant from her past, back when she had time for luxuries like her own writing, Hilda Donaldson had moved on to questions the reader needed to ask themselves. There were a *lot* of questions, an interrogation room's worth. Were these related to the previous "steps"? But to ask anything at this point risked revealing her inattention. This would set Erica up for a headache when tasked with turning the transcripts into something coherent, but there wasn't much else she could do.

Erica took another deep breath, intending to focus again on the black T-shirt. But now, she saw only polished wood. The T-shirt was gone. And while it seemed that things shouldn't just slip on their own—not without some catalyst—as the spouse of a geologist she knew that nothing was as stable as we liked to believe. The Earth was constantly shifting beneath our feet.

Yet after the call, Erica found no black material puddled on the hardwood floor as expected. There was absolutely no sign of the T-shirt.

"Hey, Joel? There *was* a shirt on the back of that chair, right?"

Joel stalked into the hall in a sweatshirt and pajama pants, his posture hunched and features clenched and brooding. Clapping "buddy" Daddy was no more—not for her, at least. "I'm trying to work *and* get our kids through the school day. Sorry if I didn't pick up!"

Were his own children really such a burden? If he registered this question on her face, he ignored it. Beyond that, the span of a single hour was hardly "the school day." And beyond *that*, or maybe the real issue at hand, was that Erica's original question wasn't some veiled scold. It was simply a request to help her explain away the T-shirt's unsettling disappearance. But the appearance of that story snippet was also unsettling, perhaps even more so. She felt so far removed from the woman she once was that she couldn't even remember writing it.

The next day, Joel knocked over a tray of buttons, marbles, thumbtacks, and paperclips arranged in bowls on the coffee table, accessible for Dylan's Montessori sorting activity. "I put my feet up." Joel shrugged as he returned them to the carpet. But he made no move to clean up after himself. Instead, he picked up the remote and turned on the television.

Joel was under significant pressure at his job, she got that. As long as his next contract was approved, he would finally become staff. This had seemed like a sure thing pre-pandemic. And now, if it wasn't approved—if Erica had to take on more clients as the primary breadwinner, well, she was already doing a portion of the bread-winning, and he was doing no housework whatsoever. He was exerting the absolute minimum of care for their children, and begrudgingly at that, so she didn't see how a reshuffling of their duties could possibly work.

Erica exhaled, hard and fast, like blowing out candles through her nose. As she did, the red, blue, and yellow paperclips and buttons shimmered away. To where, she had no clue, but she felt certain they had to go somewhere. And with them gone, she felt freer, lighter somehow—perhaps due simply to the fact that it was one less thing to clean or dust or shove into a drawer.

Yet when she looked to Joel, he was still flipping through channels like nothing had happened. She considered how the shimmering suggested oil in a puddle of water, two things that didn't mix, that shouldn't really be there, like that, together.

The next day, Friday, the bathroom door flew open as she was trying to divide her attention between a client's manuscript and

Penny's class story time via Zoom. "Have you seen my shampoo?" Joel demanded, the shower running in the background.

Erica had. The bottle was wedged in the caddy in such a way that it had oozed all over her conditioner. Her resentment had bubbled up, and— "It seems to have disappeared."

"Okay." He set his jaw and cinched the towel tighter over his paunch. "Where would I find more?"

"In the hall closet, most likely."

Joel opened the closet, dripping water on the hardwood floor. He didn't get it. Erica cleared her throat and spoke emphatically. "It seems that things have been *disappearing*. As in, 'poof! *Gone*.'"

"Abracadabra!" Dylan joined in from the bedroom.

Joel's expression in response was almost threatening, startling at the very least. Did he think this was some passive-aggressive thing, like, if he didn't pick up after himself, she was going to "disappear" his stuff?

"This isn't some game, Joel!" But he'd already returned to the shower, and now, at the mention of "game," Dylan came out to play Go Fish. And while taking this hour out of time she already didn't have surely contributed to their mother-son bond, as well as Dylan's sense of self-worth and his overall mental development, it meant falling farther behind with her paid work.

That weekend into week four of the lockdown, the disappearing continued. Erica's temper would flare, and the item taking the brunt of it went . . . Elsewhere. The sneakers Joel left in the middle of the living room for her to trip on, the loveseat he'd pulled out from the wall to get at a socket and left jutting out into the room, the damp towels he flung on the bathroom floor. Her impulse felt as involuntary as belching or snatching up dirty dishes as she moved through a room. She wasn't trying to do it, but she also wasn't holding back. And she imagined that with every material object lost, something was returned to her in spirit. It felt that way. It really did.

By mid-week Erica was even somewhat buoyant going into the evening meal, for once. And Joel initiated conversation, which he hadn't done in a while. It probably helped that the children were uncharacteristically subdued, no whining or tantrums (yet). Perhaps with the disappearances they sensed something was amiss, or maybe they were afraid of their father right now, which seemed just as plausible. Yet tonight she felt hopeful enough that she imagined Joel more himself, or more like the man she thought she'd married—a patient, caring guy she could talk to, with a decent sense of humor and intelligent interests.

"It sure will be a relief when the project review is completed."

"You must be really busy." It was a question, really, but Joel hadn't been taking kindly to those. Yet he seemed more distant than busy, from what she could tell. He crept into bed well after she'd fallen asleep and slept in until his first meeting (if he had one) or until she woke him to watch the kids for hers.

"It's the waiting that's killing me. The not-knowing."

"So, you're not that busy, then?"

"What's with the third degree?"

Erica raised her eyebrows, then took a deep, calming breath so that everyone could enjoy the meal without anything disappearing. When he'd left the house for work, they'd kept the same relative schedule, at least. And with Dylan finally starting school, she had gotten used to something like her own space for some portion of the day. And now, somehow, he'd made this space for himself—or took her space—because now she had nothing.

"What's a third degree?" Penny ripped off a thick leaf and scooped up a good teaspoon of mayonnaise.

Erica considered some elaborate explanation of the degrees one got after college, terminating with the third, the PhD, which her father had obtained in the geological sciences—but it would cost her more effort than she had energy. And it wouldn't explain Joel's harsh tone, which was at the heart of Penny's question. *Why is Daddy mad? Is he mad at you? Is he mad at us?*

Dylan pushed rice around on his plate. "Do you want more chicken?"

"I have rice."

"I see that." Erica also saw that Penny wasn't actually eating her artichoke. She was plucking a leaf, using it as a mayonnaise scoop, then depositing it in an uneaten pile with the rest. Erica decided it was only fair to ignore this as well.

After dinner, Joel couldn't find his cholesterol pills. Erica stood over his shoulder, trying to help him look, when he spun around. "Are you trying to kill me, now?"

Erica stepped back but otherwise held her ground. "Don't be ridiculous."

She'd known for weeks now that things would need to change. And now that they were, in fact, changing, she had no idea where this was all headed. When Erica was honest with herself, she knew her marriage hadn't been okay for some time. *Each day is a new one!* she'd been telling herself, at least since Dylan was born—which was far easier to believe when everyone left the house. She suspected Joel was keeping secrets. There were the beers until late after work, well after she put the kids to bed, presumably with colleagues he was hoping to impress in the interest of that staff position she'd been hearing so much about. But maybe an affair, or a porn addiction—whatever might account for their nonexistent sex life. She didn't press too closely around the shape of his disappointments and anxieties. Why should she, when he cared nothing for her own? And so, her resentment had now become a weapon, certainly, but was it a deadly one? She really didn't know.

"You've already 'disappeared' my deodorant and my comb. Where did you hide them, Erica? Or did you throw them away? You did!" He seemed to take her blinks as affirmation. "You know what, I'm going for a walk."

He'd clearly meant to storm out, but he couldn't find the jacket he normally wore and had to fish around in the hall closet before yanking out some ugly brown thing instead. She imagined teenagers driving by and yelling incoherent insults—and in response, the jacket disappeared even as he slid in an arm. But Joel just continued out the door as if nothing she did could touch him. And when he returned twenty minutes later, he smelled herbal and earthy, slightly reminiscent of a skunk.

The next week continued in a similar fashion, and the one after that—with Joel getting himself worked up enough to warrant "walking it off" after dinner. She cared far less about the marijuana than his baseless irritation with her that he used for his excuse—the *childishness* of it. And each time, something would disappear, as if following him out the door.

More than once, she'd fantasized about doing the same.

NOW, THREE WEEKS INTO Erica's developing powers and six weeks into pandemic lockdown, Erica had come to accept this chasm in their marriage as the "new normal" everyone was talking about. Things disappeared inside it, sure, but the world was a crazy place right now, for everyone. Even those smiling people on social media showing off their sourdough loaves looked dazed, like trying to avoid looking directly at something staring them down off camera.

Joel had spent the day shut up in Dylan's former room, yet again. Doing what, she didn't know. Sure, details of the proposal were still being hammered out, and there were important scheduled conferences, even impromptu meetings. But besides that, was he on call for geological advice? Researching other job opportunities? She suspected he was just sitting in there, surfing the internet while binging on the potato chips and cheese puffs that kept appearing despite the agreed-upon "no junk food in the house" rule, while leaving her to hold things down on her own.

"I'm going to the store, Joel!" Erica yelled in the general direction of Dylan's former room. She'd showered and looked presentable enough. Her T-shirt was clean, and her hair was brushed. It had gotten a little long and uneven—just past her chin now, but she wasn't quite brave enough to attempt a haircut herself. "The kids are done with school for the day, but make sure they don't burn the house down, huh?"

Erica tried to straddle the line between arriving late enough at the supermarket to avoid a line and early enough that something might still be left on the shelves. The sweet spot was just after Penny's school ended for the day.

"Will do!" Joel shouted back, his voice harsh with disdain.

Erica's jaw clenched as she reached for a mask in the basket on the entryway table. And just like that, there was only the mask she now held in her hand. The basket and remaining masks had gone elsewhere. She stood for a moment at the front door, waiting for sounds of Joel getting up off his ass. She tried not to look at the partial handprint in miniature to one side that it would be left to her to remove, as the walls themselves bore down with the equal and opposite force of her frustrations, pinning her with a sense of obligation that left her almost paralyzed.

It was at that moment that she felt something sharp dig into her shin.

"Ow!" She lifted her foot and hit her son with it. "Dylan! Did you just bite my leg?"

"Yes." Her four-year-old smiled shyly, like he'd done something cute. Just the disarming smile Erica needed to take her rage down a notch. And now, guilt swept over Erica instead. Because what if she'd stared at the wall for another two or three more seconds? What if she'd directed the brunt of her rage at the cause of the sharp pain, without knowing what it was?

"What did your teacher tell you about biting?" Before lockdown, Dylan had bitten another preschooler. The bite was gentle, luckily, the classmate's skin unmarked.

"No biting other kids." Dylan hung his head.

"Or adults. No biting *anyone*."

"Yeah, no biting, Dylan," Penny now joined in.

"Just biting food," Dylan told his big sister.

"That's right. Teeth are for chewing your food." Penny nodded emphatically.

"Yes! Because I bampire horse!"

"Dylan, honey, we've talked about the difference between real and pretend, right?"

"I play-pretend bampire horse."

"Okay. But we don't hurt others when we play-pretend. No biting. No hitting. Right?"

Dylan shrugged. "Sometimes." Then he wandered off.

"He's giving himself a time-out," Penny explained. This was new, her son acting out just to earn himself some space. She certainly couldn't blame him.

Finally, she heard Joel open the door, his footsteps in the hall. She hugged Penny tight.

"I'm going to the store. Be good for your dad. I'll see you both in a bit."

If only she could disappear. The thought came to Erica in the third person like this, like Joel's thought, projected. Yet it didn't sound so bad, did it? Disappearing, then reappearing somewhere else? Erica slipped out the front door and hurried down the front path to the sidewalk as if chased.

Across the street, work on the neighbor's front yard renovation had been paused for weeks, long enough that the recent rain had sprouted tender shoots of grass to create the appearance of an unmarked grave in a meadow, in front of their Spanish-style bungalow. She suspected the mound was a by-product of the digging, but could it be the intended effect? Most head-scratching of all was a significant pile of empty nursery pots against the porch, when there was no sign of anything having been planted. Ronnie and Yvette didn't have kids, so she'd think they'd have more time on their hands, not less. Not that Erica was resentful of her kids—they were good kids, but she did feel a stab of jealousy at the thought of being in that way unfettered. Yet this was Joel's fault, not theirs. It was his lack of help, his anger at the slightest thing adding to her workload and overall stress. Erica hated this internal monologue, hated herself when she heard her own complaining, downright depressing tone. *I'm really not okay*, she thought. *I'm not coping well. I've become a monster.*

It wasn't until Erica fastened her seatbelt that the tingling started, lightly enough to resemble the conception of a strange, newly dawning thought, something like goosebumps.

At the supermarket, Erica discovered, as she did each time, a world grown too bright, almost hyper-realistic, everything a reminder of her biological frailty. And so, she attributed the strange fluttery feeling in her chest and the tingling along her arms to anxiety.

At the end of the pasta aisle, an old man peeked hairy nostrils over a blue paper mask. "Keep it covered, old man," Erica muttered, her words muffled beneath her own mask, which was of course why the man did not look up. Instead, he reached for a pale red box and shook it near one hairy ear. At just past 3 p.m., it was one of only a few remaining, off-brand, the packaging unfamiliar.

The man nodded, then put the box in his cart. He reached for a second box and shook this one too. But now, he furrowed his brow. He returned it to the shelf. She did not know this trick or what it might reveal about the box's contents, but mostly she was appalled that he *put the box back* for someone else to grab. If she were to pick up that box directly after him, they may as well have shaken hands. No worse than the flu, people said. But who wanted the flu? The flu was horrible.

And just like that, on pure impulse, Erica ducked down and slipped in front of the man. She grabbed the one remaining box he had not yet contaminated with potentially virus-laden hands and put it in her cart. And now the man looked up, blinking at her as if she had just appeared. In a sense she had.

Erica took a moment to apply hand sanitizer from her purse before turning her cart abruptly in the opposite direction, toward the canned veggies, which she did not normally use—although perhaps they would come in handy if the supply chain really was breaking down, despite the media's confident claims of hoarding as the reason shelves were near-cleared-out after noon. The cart's wheels glitched, and she looked down to see a giant black arrow stuck to the linoleum, pointing the way ahead. She saw now that the floorplan of the grocery store had been turned into a giant boardgame. How had she missed this before?

Along this aisle, there were other packaged goods, like broths and soups, even canned beans and tomatoes, which she might actually use. But that selection was limited. She added a few split pea soups to her cart, a super-organic bonemeal broth that was four times the price of anything else. She placed the last two cans of tomatoes in her cart. They were the size of her head, but she could freeze any excess.

Erica turned onto one of the main thoroughfares again, which was agnostic, no designated direction set. She turned down the baking aisle, where her progress was halted by a young couple musing over types of flours. They, too, were fondling packages, holding them up to their faces as they pulled down their masks. Erica waited for them to continue along, at least—to treat the aisle like a line and continue wheeling their carts at an even pace like a conveyer belt taking them through the store, thereby maintaining a proper social distance.

"Excuse me!" Erica finally announced.

"What?" the man craned his large head toward the woman, who lowered her polka-dotted mask. "Potato flour. Have you tried it? The package says—"

"Seriously?" Erica huffed. She reversed her cart with as much rattling as she could muster, with no response from them still. Instead, the tingling down Erica's arms intensified, and she barely avoided running into an older woman coming down the main aisle at a surprising clip.

Erica imagined now that she was slowly disappearing, popping out of this reality and into the next and back again. This would mean that for brief moments her cart would appear to be moving of its own accord, a ghost-cart haunting the aisles. And in this world turned upside down, no one would even notice! Inertia, they'd assume, or uneven floors. A particularly strong air current. Because who had the bandwidth to consider the paranormal on top of the sci-fi dystopia everyday life had become?

Erica took a sharp right down the empty paper goods aisle, intending to cut over to produce, when a man pushed his cart against the arrow and right at her. She continued forward, and he likewise continued, passing much too close. She could feel the air his body offset. She held her breath, and as he passed, for just an instant, she could see his body, but not her own—no solidity to the arm that he should be skimming—and she couldn't feel his touch.

But, no, her arm was there. Her cart was there. And now, suddenly, he wasn't. She remembered one time in elementary school, experimenting with modes of breath, and she'd hyperventilated until things had started to go dark. Her mother had taken her to a doctor. "Are you breathing like this?" And the doctor demonstrated the fast, shallow action she'd been engaging in all that day previous. "Well, stop it," the doctor had said.

That must be all there was to it—the heightened anxiety most everyone was experiencing during the first global pandemic in 100 years. She just needed to stop it.

At checkout, the cashier looked past her while scanning groceries, as if wondering where she might have scurried off to. Only when it was time to pay did he make eye contact, the corners creased like he was smiling. "Why, hello!" He projected this clearly through the fabric of his mask, followed by something incomprehensible. Erica smiled, then realized her mouth was not visible. Her smile was not sincere, or practiced enough, to touch her eyes.

The bagger held up the off-brand macaroni box it seemed she had left in the cart. He wore opaque plastic gloves. "Is this yours, ma'am?"

His question made her reconsider. Erica shook her head. But dry goods *were* currently hard to come by right now. "No, you know what? I'll take it."

"You want it?" The cashier held the box now.

"Yes, I—could you just . . . give it a little shake?" Erica knew to thump a watermelon, and how to feel for an apple's crispness—the trick of pulling at a pineapple's crown. But she didn't know this one.

The cashier seemed unfazed by this request. He held it up to his ear just like the old man had. "Oh, yeah. No. You don't want this one."

"I don't. Okay, then." But now, she noticed something distinctly strange about the box, compelling, a strange pixelation or shimmering, perhaps initiated by the shaking. It was almost like the box was both here and also not.

"Okay you do . . . or you don't want it?"

In the end, Erica left with the box. She loaded the groceries in the back, then dialed Kristin, her best friend from college, as soon as she started the engine, the ringing picked up and projected over the Accord's speakers via Bluetooth.

"Hey, Erica, what's up?"

"I'm disappearing," she blurted out.

"Join the club."

"No, I mean, like actually—poof! Disappearing."

"Motherhood, kids, the sacrifice. Am I a nanny or a mom? A housekeeper or a wife? Who am I anymore? Right?"

"Sure, but—"

"I sometimes imagine, when I walk by houses, all the basements and backrooms and sheds and garages where a woman or child might be locked up. And I listen for pleas for help or scuffles or muffled screams that I might otherwise fail to notice. I've told you this, right?"

"Yeah . . ."

"Okay, well, I just pulled up at the studio. Call you later?" Kristin taught a few Pilates classes a week, albeit virtually now. She said it made up for all the time she spent sitting in front of a screen.

"Sure." Was Kristin saying that neither of them had it so bad because neither of their homes was an actual prison? Yet knowing Kristin, she more likely was implying that it wasn't so far off. She preferred to push and unsettle, to get people thinking differently. It was Kristin who'd first posed the question, *Who is the vampire horse in your life?*

Really, the idea had originated with the kids. She'd taken them on an afternoon hike at least three months ago now, and Dylan had dug in his heels about returning, complaining that the way back took too long. So, she let him throw rocks into the creek until the sun lowered enough that the air grew cold, Penny complained, and finally Dylan assented. By the time they reached the trailhead, it was on the darker side of dusk. Yet as they were walking out, more than one person on horseback ventured in. This seemed odd enough to Erica, and then Penny pronounced, "There goes another vampire horse." Somehow, this made perfect sense in her seven-year-old brain, which stuck with Erica, sparking her imagination. The rider as familiar, of course, but what was it they did in the forested canyons at night? While the concept of vampirism was not at all peaceful, in her mind's eye was a quiet clearing at the center of a grove of stately oaks that absolutely was. Erica still wasn't entirely sure what this meant.

Walking back up to the house with a bag in either arm, she felt a breeze gust through her. And when she reached the porch, the bags dropped out of her arms as if she'd suddenly let go. Only she hadn't. She blinked, and when she looked to where they should have fallen, there was only the box of pasta sitting there in front of the large flowering bush on the other side of the railing. The box appeared to be strobing, like an image trapped in some loop of code. But the bush was also now bursting with yellow, so vibrant as to be almost blinding. She would have sworn there was not so much as a bud on it when she'd left. Also, she felt preternaturally calm, something akin to contentment. It was nice here, she thought, which was strange since she wasn't somewhere else. She had simply returned home.

Erica noticed a potted ranunculus blooming to one side of the door in oranges and pinks. It was her favorite flower, gifted to her by Yvette from across the street for Easter a couple weeks ago. She'd left it with a note at the door, and Erica had completely forgotten about it. Of course, she would only notice it when coming home, yet someone must have watered it in the meantime. She glanced across the street as the question began to form in her mind, and it seemed that while she was at the store, somehow, in the span of an hour, Ronnie and Yvette had suddenly finished their yard. They'd hilled up dirt on either side of a front path they'd put in, then planted it with an assortment of succulents and cacti—aloe and firesticks and echeveria with their artichoke-shaped clusters, a couple agave presenting thick swords. A shiver made its way through Erica, now, because she didn't just feel different. Things *were* different.

The tingling in Erica's arms persisted. She rubbed her shoulder, which felt solid enough, even as the tingling continued up it and across her chest. But it wasn't painful. It didn't *feel* like a heart attack. Maybe it just felt like disappearing. She didn't truly believe this was happening. But she didn't *not* believe it, either.

Erica entered the house quietly, the air stagnant and warm, heavy with some underlying, vaguely unpleasant musk and a slight scent of lavender dish soap. Yet the house appeared as it had weeks ago: that is, full. A pile of laundry waited to be folded on the loveseat—on top that cute jumper of Penny's she hadn't seen in weeks, Joel's favorite striped shirt; the ottoman with a Lego castle on display; the entertainment center and bookshelf; the entryway carpet. And then, that shimmer. She blinked, and everything was as she'd left it little more than an hour ago. That is, half-empty, emptying. There was still the sofa, the entry way and coffee table, and one standing lamp. Everything else had gone . . . Elsewhere.

Erica's footsteps now echoed faintly against the hardwood floor. Yet Dylan had not come running to throw his chubby little arms around her knees, which meant no one had noticed she was home. Erica closed her eyes, enjoying what may be the last moment she'd have to herself until she went to the store again. She took a deep breath and imagined herself at a writer's retreat on a private beach or a treehouse resort, sitting around a bonfire under the stars or along a table on a wide veranda. *The vampire horse,* they'd tell her, *feels timeless somehow. Or time-ly,* someone else would interject. *Is it a commentary on current politics?* Everyone would laugh, then—not at her, but with her—at the absurdity of this era in which they were now living and how the vampire horse really was the perfect thing.

But this fantasy just served to remind her that she hadn't written down a single word of it, or of anything else for that matter, since the pandemic had hit.

"Honey?"

Erica sighed. But it had been a while since she'd heard a term of endearment pass Joel's lips, so she turned her head in the direction of his voice, albeit grudgingly.

"You are home. Good news! They approved the project! I'm going to be staff! Finally! I'll fill out all the paperwork on Monday. We're doing a Zoom-ebration later. Do we have any champagne?"

"If I'd known. I just came back from the store."

"Do you need help putting things away?" She saw straight through to his selfishness. He just wanted an outlet for his nervous energy.

"There might be a couple bags on the porch." There also might not be. Erica found she just didn't care anymore. It didn't matter. After all this time they'd been in limbo, after all the slack she'd given him—she'd simply let go of the line. Oops.

"I did the dishes."

"How nice." She attempted a smile. "Why don't you see about those bags, huh?"

Doing the dishes was the first chore he'd lifted a finger to complete since . . . she honestly couldn't recall.

Joel returned much too quickly with the bags. "I'm sorry if I've been distracted lately."

IF? Distracted?? But Erica didn't have the space to get into it now if she wanted to. "I've got that five p.m call I told you about. I need to get ready." She'd agreed to go late for Hilda Donaldson since the woman's schedule had changed, but she really did need to stop being so goddamn accommodating. "Can you keep an eye on the kids?"

"Sure. I'll pop out for a bottle after."

Erica felt that too-familiar feeling bubble up. It wasn't okay for Joel to treat her with complete contempt and disdain, then pretend that everything was suddenly fine. Oh, and never mind him celebrating with colleagues in the other room when she was the one who deserved that champagne toast. He owed her an apology at the very least, a significant one, formal and heartfelt and reflective—with all the parts. No simple "I'm sorry." This apology would be the necessary first step. Then, he would need to take on chores—*daily* chores—not just taking the garbage down to the curb each week. Then—yeah, there were already too many steps. She didn't see Joel successfully completing even the first one.

At 4:55 p.m., Erica sat down and logged in to the conference call. A light-saber-like sound came from Penny's room, as well as the motor-like noise Dylan made to accompany a toy car. The door was closed, and as long as it stayed that way, these sounds weren't so distracting that Erica couldn't concentrate. At exactly 5:00 p.m., Hilda logged in.

"Hello, Hilda! How are you? Ready to get started with Chapter . . . the chapter?" Erica realized that she had no idea what chapter they were on, let alone what her project was about. She was a bit fuzzy headed like she sometimes got when angry, but she felt overall calm. Erica had pulled up the documents ahead of time like she had the past couple weeks after the shirt incident, sure to have them ready. But now, they were nowhere on her desktop. In "recents" the only document to appear was titled "Vampire Horse." This couldn't be right, yet she opened it anyway.

After her mother disappeared, Pearl became the keeper of things inside the house. She still imagined the walls forming a distinct barrier, which she mistook for security. Open the door and you're outside, where anything could happen. Close it, and you're inside, safe and sound. And so, she shut the door, didn't think too much about the animals that dug and bit and attacked each other. Some for food; others for sport. Nature had an order to it, a base, vicious one, perhaps, but an order all the same.

Inside, it was up to Pearl to maintain this order. And if she let one thing disappear and then another, and things started moving around willy-nilly, at what point would it become impossible to redirect, to turn it all back around? Even now, items kept disappearing, and then reappearing where they just didn't belong! Or did they . . . ? Because what if this arrangement Pearl had been taught to impose was all wrong? Would this explain what happened to her mother?

The cursor sat at the end, blinking. Cursor. Curse. Erica felt the tingling down her arms again. She had not written these lines, yet here they were.

"Erica?"

What if the house were haunted? And what if she were the ghost? "Yes?"

"Oh, I thought I heard a click. I thought we were disconnected."

"I'm still here." In Erica's periphery, she could make out the pasta box on the counter. It was shimmery, translucent, iridescent like a fish. She couldn't tell if it were coming or going. The connection with the client was just as bad.

"Good! So, like I was saying . . . certain challenges that men don't. Because . . . leans more conservative . . . battling biases about women working outside the home, and . . . sexism, frankly. So, the first . . . a coach, a female mentor and . . . this woman is supporting not undermining your efforts, which we'll talk more about in the next chapter."

Hilda Donaldson was breaking up, and the transcript would be virtually unusable, although sometimes the recording could be fine regardless of what Erica heard on her end. There was no way to know, really, how it was going to turn out, which meant that Erica should err on the side of caution.

"Hilda? Hi. Sorry to interrupt—"

Then, just like that, Erica was kicked off the internet-based call. This happened sometimes, especially when the connection was unstable. What made it feel different was the sensation like a warm current coursing down her arms, her legs, waves lapping at her neck, enveloping her torso. She could feel whatever shell was left of her slipping, falling off like old skin to be washed away. And suddenly

Hilda's voice was loud and clear. The connection not lost, it seemed, but made stronger.

"Don't be afraid to be called a 'bitch,' for one thing. Who cares? Sticks and stones, right? I know, I know. It stings, it does. So, take it to your mentor, to your therapist. But don't so much as hesitate because of it. Reclaim the word if you need to. Some women find strength in that." Hilda paused, cleared her throat. "I trust you've now arrived. So, what do you think, Erica?"

"Oh? Excuse me?"

"You've crossed over. You've arrived."

"How do you mean?"

"Elsewhere."

At first Erica assumed Hilda was simply trying to drive some connection home, which Erica couldn't grasp because she'd missed the first part of the conversation. Erica closed her eyes, pressed the lids with both palms, then blinked them open. And when she did, she saw the house was full again. Furniture, laundry, all kinds of clutter. But not Joel's things—no jacket by the front door, no sneakers, and so forth. The configuration of things within the space was different than it had been moments before, even months before.

"I've got a firm out at 1:30 p.m., my time, so let's get to it. What is it that you want to do, Erica? This is your chance. You want to take what you've learned and start your own business, or make a real go at freelance? Or maybe you have a creative goal?"

Where was Hilda located that she was four hours behind California? Regardless, Erica had clearly lost her mind. Or she was dead. She'd had an aneurism when she saw that T-shirt flicker over the back of the chair—*that* was the flickering, her brain going offline, not the shirt. What she'd experienced as the past three weeks was just her last dream spiraling out.

Erica pinched her arm, even though she hated when people did that in books. She'd never once in a dream had the urge to pinch herself, which meant that the urge itself should be an indicator that one was not dreaming. And sure enough, she felt the pressure of pinching flesh between thumb and pointer finger as well as the sting of being pinched, just as she knew she would. She needed to better trust herself.

Erica took a deep breath. "There is a book I've been meaning to write."

"Great. Just let me know what I can do to help, beyond the space, of course." Hilda chuckled. "What's the book about?"

"It's a children's book. About a vampire horse."

"Well, divorce is always a timely topic!"

Erica hesitated to correct her. If the woman had the power to make whatever this was possible . . . but then Erica also had significant powers, as she was discovering. "So, how does this work?" she asked instead.

"You take the time you need to get what you need done. I'll check in every few days. We'll take it from there."

"Sounds good." And also unrealistic. Definitely too good to be true.

"I know you'll put this opportunity to good use. I believe in you, Erica." And with that, Hilda hung up.

Erica couldn't remember the last time someone had said something so positive to her, so inspirational, so *nice*. It filled her with a warm, fuzzy determination to use her time productively. Her laptop was right here in front of her, and there was no one to shame her for not cleaning up. No kids to feel guilty about neglecting. Although there were kids, her kids . . . they just weren't here. *Stop it, Erica. This is your time to focus on yourself.* And while she wasn't sure if that voice came from inside herself, or just outside, the sentiment was one she felt determined to embrace.

She got started. She opened Word to that first blank page with the blinking cursor, and before the anxiety of it could take hold she typed, "The Vampire Horse Chronicles" (even though the title would probably change) and her name. Then she wrote the first few lines.

The horses didn't leave the stables until nightfall, when the familiar arrived to sweep aside a pile of straw and pull back the hidden door leading to the mausoleum beneath. Around her, the gentle fall of horses breathing, their light, whinnying snores. Below her, everything was still.

To call her a "familiar" was too telling, of course. Erica would flesh out the character and work on letting things unfold as she drafted. But she still had questions she'd need to answer. Did the vampire horses feed on horses, or did they just hide out under the stables? Were the riders the familiars, or did the familiar switch the regular horse out with a vampire unbeknownst to the riders? So, the rider would take the vampire horse out to the canyon and the clearing, and then . . . the vampire horse would turn on them? Of course, that would mean the vampire horses fed on humans.

Speaking of food, Erica got up to inspect the kitchen. The cupboards were stocked, and the refrigerator full. And now, the thought of making a meal for herself, with no regard to anyone else's like or dislikes—well, it was a lot more compelling than forcing her way through the questions her subconscious just needed to chew on anyway. There were fresh tomatoes, garlic, anchovies, herbs, and all the black pepper she could handle. Extra virgin olive oil, of course, fresh parmesan. They ate pasta often enough at home, but not *good* pasta. There was an assortment of wild mushrooms in the crisper, even a small piece of truffle. *Well.* And the wine rack was stocked with good stuff, not the under-$10-at-Trader-Joe's variety. A green salad, a couple glasses of a rich, earthy cab, and a plate of pasta, and Erica was ready for bed. She'd start again, fresh, in the morning.

Erica slept better than she had in months. The bedroom here was furnished like her room when she and Joel had first started dating, so when she tucked herself into her double bed that night, then threw off the flowered quilt, she could almost believe that her life had just continued forward on the trajectory it might have assumed if she had not married and had children. Even though, given how she'd come to arrive here, that could hardly be the case.

She brewed coffee first thing, then sat down again at her laptop. She'd had this thought that perhaps the vampire horses ate children, which seemed like it could be too much, but Hansel and Gretel, right? If witches could eat children, why not horses? So. The familiars would sacrifice the children to the horses, why? What would they get out of it? Immortality was too easy, and a curse when you really thought about it. *And why horses?* Kristin had pressed her on this. For one, Erica now thought, those teeth could crush a skull like a melon. She also liked the idea of beasts of burden turning on the people they'd been forced to serve. There was also that whole Freudian thing with little girls and horses as a stand-in for the male body that she felt pointed in an appropriately ominous direction.

It seemed the pieces were finally beginning to fall into place.

Yet Erica found herself distracted by the faint sound of voices coming from the other room. She got up to investigate and found herself in what would be the room Penny now shared with Dylan in the other world, the real world. A gentle murmuring came through the air vent. Penny reading to Dylan, maybe? Or the two of them quietly discussing what happened to their mother while their father did whatever he did in the office/Dylan's old room. She felt a pang of guilt, but her absence was necessary for their father to step up. She wasn't the only parent, and it was unfair of Joel to act like she was. Besides, she'd go back, eventually.

It was much roomier in here without beds. There was only the round carpet in the shades of purple Penny loved and a small stack of books, an assortment of Legos and other toys, but no shelves. No drapes. She stood there a moment, looking out at the mountains and the sun cresting over the neighbor's oak tree when she saw Ronnie and Yvette exit their front door, outfitted to do some gardening, a brimmed hat virtually hiding Yvette's face. They waved when they saw her. Erica waved back. Yet she had imagined this alternative space would be all her own. Ronnie and Yvette continued waving, until she realized they were waving her over.

Erica would go be neighborly, and then right after she'd get back to work.

"Erica!" Yvette exclaimed. She was the outgoing one, Ronnie more reserved.

"Great to see you!" Ronnie backed her up. They shouted from across the street as she made her way down the path, then stood in the gutter. They stopped there too. Whether this was due to the pandemic or to some unspoken rules of this place, Erica wasn't sure. She simply felt that this was where she should stop.

"We haven't seen you or Joel in . . . I don't know, weeks probably?" Ronnie looked to Yvette. Their arm was around her now, and she nodded, brow furrowed, as if with concern.

"Everything okay over there?" Her tone was joking. Yet.

"Ha ha. We haven't seen you either. Everything okay over *there*?"

Yvette took Ronnie's hand resting over her shoulder and smiled up at them. "We've really just gotten in touch with each other these last few weeks, you know?"

Never mind that they had to be pushing fifty or so, that was something you could do with no children underfoot, and with a giving, loving partner. "I like what you've done with the yard." Erica changed the subject.

"We do too! We have time to garden now, and for landscaping!"

"Yeah, our yard could use some attention." It really could. There was the flowering bush by the porch, and that was pretty much it. They'd let the lawn die, intending to pull it out and cash in on one of those water-saving rebates, but neither she nor Joel had the time or energy to do the work and paying someone to do it never came together. But now. Well.

"Are Joel and the kids . . . somewhere?" Ronnie asked.

"They're visiting his parents." This lie just rolled out. "I came back a little early."

"Oh, okay." Yvette didn't push, didn't ask when they might be coming back, or why Erica came back without them, which she appreciated since the when and where of things now seemed tangled. She was no longer sure that the other version was the "real" one.

"Well, I'll see you two around, then!"

"Yes! You will!"

Erica went around to the garage, pulled out all the tools she'd need to take out the lawn. She changed into work clothes and dug in, tearing up the brown clumped sod with a pickaxe until her shoulders hurt and her nostrils were coated with dirt.

WHEN HILDA CHECKED IN a few evenings later, Erica was enjoying a meal of miso-glazed salmon over sautéed bok choy with rice and a seaweed salad. It was amazing, what she could put together with the proper ingredients and the time to really focus on a meal's preparation.

"That sounds amazing," Hilda agreed. "So how is your divorce going?"

"You mean my book? I thought I'd take a few days to decompress, you know. Let thoughts percolate. I've been busy taking out the front lawn."

"I bet that's therapeutic."

"It is. You know, it really is."

"Are you ready for a visit from your kids?"

"Oh." So soon. "Yes, I would love to see Dylan and Penny."

Erica felt a bit apprehensive after the call, she had to admit, but she did her best to enjoy the rest of her meal. When she got up to rinse off her plate, she heard a commotion in the other room, and sure enough, both kids came running out. They were already in their pajamas, which meant they should be fed, she hoped. "What a surprise! How did you two get here?"

"Mommy!" both kids yelled as Penny crashed into her first, grabbing her around the waist. "We had ice cream for dinner!"

And while this brought all her irritation with Joel right back, it was distant. It affected her far less. Erica burned through their sugar rush, leading them in an extensive game of Simon Says with plenty of jumping jacks and so forth, intended to wear them out before moving into story time. Erica was eager to try out some of the ideas she'd been hashing. "What's scarier than a horse?"

"A vampire horse!" Penny and Dylan responded in unison. They lay on either side of her, tucked into the big bed. "A slumber party," she'd called it.

"Yes! So, once upon a time there was a vampire horse, a whole herd of vampire horses in fact, and they fed on the blood of children. The vampire horse would appear outside a child's window and say, 'I want to suck your blood,' and the child could say either 'Okay' or 'Too bad. No way. Get lost!'" Even though this wasn't at all the book she was writing, which was interesting to realize. "So, at the first window, the horse tap-tap-tapped with his hoof and a little boy looked out. The vampire horse said, 'I want to suck your blood.' And the little boy said, 'No way!'"

"Why would you say okay?" Penny asked. Her expression was highly skeptical, which caused Erica's chest to swell with pride.

Erica realized then that the key to a good children's book was teaching a lesson about how people *should* live in this world. Not how they actually *did*, which was for more advanced age groups—coming of age and all that. It seemed that maybe the vampire horse was a cautionary tale, then, about why little girls shouldn't just agree. "Sometimes, people are taught to be agreeable and polite, no matter what. They do what others want even when it might hurt them or otherwise put them in danger."

Penny and Dylan tilted their heads up at her in near-perfect unison. Maybe the vampire horse was a coming-of-age story after all.

"Like when Mommy agrees to do all the housework even when Daddy should be helping. The extra stress can . . . lead to health problems." Erica could hear how hollow this must sound to them.

"But what does that have to do with vampires?" Penny puckered her lips.

"Let's try a different story," Erica suggested. Predictability—and the repetition that underscored it—that was what children found satisfying. "Once upon a time, there was a little boy who called himself 'El Tiburon,' or 'The Shark," because all he wanted was to bite things. He loved the feel of objects held between his teeth. The soft give of cardboard. The tappity-tap of enamel on metal, the lighter tick-tick-tick of teeth against plastic." She waxed poetic on the textures, including as much onomatopoeia as she could, until Dylan's eyelids fluttered closed and she heard Penny lightly snoring.

The vampire horse was proving to be a harder sell than she'd anticipated.

Erica recalled a time when Joel would hold her until she fell asleep, and it felt like safety, like where she was supposed to be—that strong, warm embrace, that feeling of love cocooning them. He'd been in grad school for geoscience when they'd met at a party her first year teaching. He was tall and more muscular than she'd expected a scientist to be, with deep brown eyes that would seem to gleam, just slightly, when they fell on her. And with the kids here, and the unpleasant version of him now absent, Erica could almost remember that initial attraction—how enthralled he'd been by the formation of the Earth, its ongoing movement and settling, the tremors and shifting plates and molten magma. In hindsight, perhaps she'd imagined him transferring that enthusiasm to her. That she would become his world.

Georgia-Carolina Bridge, in a Floor-Length Dress

Amy Richerson

GEORGIA-CAROLINA BRIDGE, HIGHWAY 28, AROUND MIDNIGHT, IN A FLOOR-length dress, something like red satin, something like prom, and I think what can jazzercise give us now, and I think if I survive the jump into the river I could just swim to the shore, maybe walk home dripping wet, and I think what I would look like to the cars driving past walking down the road like that, maybe think I've escaped a mental institution or I'm just another prostitute from suburbia, maybe think I'm their ex-girlfriend's mother's ghost come back to haunt them for mistreating her daughter, maybe keep going until I get to the rough wooden cabin with the three-legged dog and the wisteria and watch the smallest speck of light come in through the morning of the cut-open window and I think

      whenever I want to die
      I think of my daughters.

      All of them—
      who bob like apples
      in the vacation bible school's silver bucket.
      I grasp one with my teeth,
      my knees in the spare, yellow grass.

What I need to live to tell her
is what my mother refuses to live to tell her daughters.
              And her mother and her mother.

We come from a long line of women who hate themselves,
        some for no reason,
        some for good reason.

I need to live to show her
how to
        hold on to the parts
        of her thighs
        that mean the most to her.

How to
play her body like a blue guitar
        or a blue canoe.

I need to hope when she sits on the low steps
of a back porch
        with the bad man blues
        or the good man blues,

she will know that I want her to live
to know that she is a miracle like everyone else.
And please

do not meet the edge of every orgasm with resistance.

For her to take
        the thousand metallic threads of each betrayal
            and embroider a quilt to shake out in the wind.

To refuse to diminish her truth for fear
of outshining her surroundings.

To live to see this very day with its
slow morning rain,
its bolted cilantro,
its green dolphin street.

I do not ask her for respect
or cathedrals,
but to wade
through the fairytales and fathers
and become at least
the woman I wanted to be.

prophecy

Jess Luna

A sleepy winter morning
They pull me from my mother
I inhale deeply

open my eyes
White starfish fluorescent lights

A dull humming
The blurry outline of a girl

Shaking

A child still
A halo of white blonde hair
The primal scent

Blood

Sweat
Salty tears
The divine scent

Love

Oxytocin
The harsh scent

Rubbing alcohol

Rubber gloves
The clean scent

My mother
Walking the tightrope of death

To give me life
Still, I turn my head

To the scent of milk
Having not yet forgotten
That I am an animal

Like my mother before me

And hers

What promises whispered

From mother

To daughter

Upon our meeting

In the tiny world

Of us

Before the world

Comes in between

And never leaves
That she would keep me safe?
I feel safe there

In her arms

For the last time

30 years pass

She does not hold me

Though I never learn

To hold myself
To speak love

Unto my own reflection
The distorted spectre

Becomes my enemy
I do not see

My mother

In her face
The over shadowing

Of dark features
The pain

Behind our eyes
Our gestures

Exaggerated
Our voice

Too loud
When I look at her

I see him
The traces

Of his outline
The man

Who hurt us both

Does she see him

when she looks at me?
Does she hear him

in my voice?
A trap

We fell into

Together

Does it hurt her

To hear me speak?
Words she cannot

Allow herself

To think

Was it her intention?
A sacrifice

I pay homage too

In the early morning hours

Before the fighting
Of the day
Commences

My purpose

to break cycles
To deliver the women
Within us to safety
Her purpose

To deliver me

Closing her eyes

Pushing me

From the nest
"Let the sky

Be a better home

Than this"
She prays
In the split second

Between falling

and flight
I look into her eyes
I make one promise
I'm coming back for you

Mom.

Contributors

BRANDEN BOYER-WHITE's debut YA graphic novel *Hollow*, co-authored with Shannon Watters (Lumberjanes), is forthcoming from Boom! Studios in fall 2022. Previously, her stories have appeared in places like *Alaska Quarterly Review*, *Third Coast*, *Los Angeles Review*, *Anthropoid*, and others. Her work has been named a runner-up for the inaugural Miami Book Fair/De Groot Prize for a Novella, been awarded a grant from the Money for Women/Barbara Deming Memorial Fund, and won the Orlando Prize, among other honors. She lives in Los Angeles.

ASHLEY MICHELLE C. is a writer, artist, and creative development teacher residing in Oaxaca de Juárez, Oaxaca, México. She is fascinated with creativity as a practice of self-love. Her work and life are based on the understanding of experience as if it were an evolving art performance—a creative personal act of discovery. Ashley takes pleasure in plunging into new experiences, taking risks, allowing herself to intimately know failure, and to fully feel delight. Her writings and work are based on approaching lifecycles, death, and pleasure with curiosity. In her poetry, essays, and videos, Ashley asks questions of her self without a necessity of finding an answer. Through this process of stream of consciousness exploration, she develops new ways of understanding the emotional, sensual, and personal impacts from her own quotidian experience. Ashley enjoys sharing her stories and encouraging others to cultivate their own creative voice.

Janet Ruth is a New Mexico ornithologist. Her writing focuses on connections to the natural world. She has recent poems in *Oddball Magazine*, *The Ocotillo Review*, *Sin Fronteras*, *Spiral Orb*, *Ekphrastic Review*, and anthologies including *Where Flowers Bloom*, honoring Ukraine (Red Penguin Collection, pending 2022), and *Moving Images: Poetry Inspired by Film* (Before Your Quiet Eyes, 2021). Her first book, *Feathered Dreams: Celebrating Birds in Poems, Stories & Images* (Mercury HeartLink, 2018), was a finalist for the 2018 NM/AZ Book Awards. See more at redstartsandravens.com/janets-poetry.

Emily Jon Tobias is an American author and poet raised in the Midwest who lives and works on the coast of Southern California. Her work has appeared in literary journals such as *Santa Clara Review*, *Talking River Review*, *Flying South Literary Journal*, *Furrow Literary Journal*, *The Opiate Magazine*, *The Ocotillo Review*, and *Jerry Jazz Musician* with work nominated for the Pushcart Prize, *Typehouse Literary Magazine*, and upcoming in *Tahoma Literary Review* and *Big Muddy*, among others. She holds an MFA in Writing from Pacific University Oregon and a bachelor's degree in creative writing from the University of Wisconsin Milwaukee.

Soraya Safavid writes from Kent Island on the Chesapeake.

Anja Semanco has published essays in *Terrain.org*, *High Desert Journal*, *Zoomorphic*, and elsewhere. Her writing has been nominated for the Pushcart Prize as well as Best American Science and Nature Writing. She holds an MA in journalism from the University of Colorado Boulder and lives in Bellingham, Washington, where she is finishing her first book of essays—a collection exploring the power of water to shape wild landscapes and internal human landscapes.

Phyn Vermin is an artist, writer, crafter, mother, and mental health worker living in Merrimack, New Hampshire. She graduated from the University of Central Florida in 2010. She interned at the *Florida Review* and has volunteered teaching writing workshops to youth in the community. Her short story "The Honesty of a Corpse" was published in the *Cypress Dome* 2011 issue 22 and won the Editor's Award for Best Nonfiction. These days she enjoys watercolor and acrylic painting, training to compete in armored combat, and hosting Taco Tuesdays as a member at MakeIt Labs in Nashua.

Tyler Wells Lynch is a writer and journalist living in Portland, Maine. His work has been published in *Permafrost, Porter House Review, Vice/ Terraform, Abyss & Apex, The Rumpus,* and *McSweeney's,* among others.

Marianne Leone is the author of *Jesse* (Simon & Schuster) and *Ma Speaks Up* (Beacon Press), and essays in the *Boston Globe, Lithub, Solstice, Coastal Living, Bark, Post Road,* and others. She had a recurring role on HBO's *The Sopranos* as Joanne Moltisanti (Christopher's mother) and acted in films by John Sayles, Larry David, Martin Scorsese, Nancy Savoca, and David O. Russell. *Jesse* is published in Italy by Nutrimenti.

Pushcart nominee **Mary Pauer**'s work in fiction and creative nonfiction can be read in *Delmarva Review, Fox Chase Review, Southern Women's Review, Chaos, Dream Streets,* to name a few, as well as in regional anthologies. She is the recipient of three Delaware Division of the Arts awards in literature as well as awards from the Delaware Press Association and the National Federation of Press Women for short fiction and her book *Traveling Moons,* and she has been the literary artist in residence at the Biggs Museum of American Art. She received her MFA in creative writing in 2010 and accepts private clients for developmental editing, intimate writer workshops, and mentoring. She can be reached at marymargaretpauer@gmail.com. When not writing she wanders her fields, attempts to train her Chow Chow puppy, and listens to the wisdom of her horses who really know what's what.

SARAH KONTOPOULOS is an emerging Seattle writer born in Vancouver, Canada, to English and Greek parents. She graduated from the University of British Columbia and earned her MA in communication disorders from the University of Oregon. Sarah's husband, Volker, and two daughters support and cheer her on in life and in writing. Their pet rabbits don't care and would like some apple now, please. Find her on IG @bunnuhledah.

BERGITA BUGARIJA was born and grew up in Zagreb, Croatia, and now lives in Pittsburgh. Her fiction appeared or is forthcoming in *Pleiades*, *Salamander*, *PANK Daily*, *Flash Fiction America* anthology, and elsewhere. She recently completed a collection of stories and is at work on a novel set in Dalmatian Hinterland.

CHARLOTTE EDSALL is an English/American writer who grew up dividing time between the misty moors and rolling green hills of South West England and the wide open skies of the North American Ozarks. She is the eldest of three and spends her free time feeding her obsession with history, folklore, and mythology. A recipient of the Felix Christopher McKean award for poetry, Charlotte has been published in the *Diamond Line* and is currently pursuing her BA in creative writing at the University of Arkansas.

VANESSA BAEHR-JONES is a writer, composer, advocate, and mother. Also, she's tired. For nearly a decade, Vanessa prosecuted child sex predators as an Assistant United States Attorney in Los Angeles and Oakland, California. A skilled trial attorney, Vanessa specialized in the complex trials of recidivist sex offenders who had traveled abroad to exploit children. A survivor of child sexual abuse herself, Vanessa left the US Department of Justice in 2021 to write a memoir about her experiences, and to launch her own law firm, Advocates for Survivors of Abuse. Vanessa lives in Oakland with her husband, two sons, a German shepherd rescue, a tabby housecat, and tumbleweeds of animal fur. You can find clips from her new musical about a young woman prosecutor and her travails in the Justice Department at www.vanessabaehrjones.com/the-musical.

FENESTRA is a singer/songwriter, writer, walker, and traveler originally from Indianapolis. She is currently working on a novel and dabbling in non-metaphorical verse that focuses on social justice, queer issues, and questioning social, economic, and relational structures.

SANDRA L. MEADE, teacher, poet, and spiritual director, lives in the piney woods north of Spokane, Washington. Her poetry can be found on The Far Field, a website of Washington poets. Her work has been published by *Stringtown, Raven Chronicles, Floating Bridge Review*, and *Washington Poetic Routes*. She received a Pushcart nomination for her poem, "Elegy for a Clown." She is bucket woman and director of Scotia House, a spiritual retreat center.

E. MARLA FELCHER has served as Cap'n of the Wild Women, a group of geographically dispersed friends who spend a couple weekends together each year, since 1998. She holds an MBA and PhD in marketing and has worked as a marketing consultant, marketing professor, investigative journalist, consumer advocate, political hell-raiser, and nonprofit social entrepreneur. Learning to write personal essays, primarily via Zoom classes during COVID, has been the toughest challenge of her career. She dedicates her essay to the memory of Jackie Nicholson, the quintessential Wild Woman.

Poet STACEY R. FORBES writes professionally for Roche Diagnostics, serving a mission to improve the lives of cancer patients. Her poem "Speaking of Trees" won first place in the 2021 Plough Poetry Prize judged by Roger McGough, and her autobiographical poem "Polaroid of a Girl from Pennsylvania" was shortlisted for the 2021 Fish Poetry Prize. Inspired by the many ways the natural world illuminates humanity, her poems are published or forthcoming in *Barren, Channel, Entropy, American Journal of Poetry, Sunlight Press, Mono, Haunted Waters Press*, and *Blue Mountain Review*. Born in the white birch woods of Pennsylvania, Stacey makes her second home in Tucson, Arizona.

ALLISON FISCHER was born in Michigan and spent many years on the move before settling in Reading, Pennsylvania. She enlisted in the Marine Corps in April 2014 and served five years on active duty, where she met her husband. Now a veteran, Allison supports her husband Dylan in his Marine Corps career. She just returned to the United States from Okinawa, Japan. Allison uses her life experiences as inspiration for her writing, with the hope that someone will be inspired to pursue their own desires.

MARIA NAZOS' poetry, translations, and essays are published in the *New Yorker*, *Cherry Tree*, *North American Review*, *Denver Quarterly*, and *Mid-American Review*. She is the author of *A Hymn That Meanders* (Wising Up Press, 2011) and the chapbook *Still Life* (Dancing Girl Press, 2016). Maria has received scholarships and fellowships from the Sewanee Writers' Conference and the Vermont Studio Center. She holds the dubious distinction of being the worst waitress on all of Cape Cod; if she spilled Pinot Noir on you, she apologizes. You can find her at www.marianazos.com.

BARBARA TYLLA spent forty years as a fiction contributor to the *St. Anthony Messenger* until 2016. A graduate of the American Academy of Dramatic Arts in 1960, she did Off-Broadway as well as summer and winter stock until her marriage in 1964. Returning to her first love, writing, she began contributing to the religious and inspirational field. Her short stories won three Catholic Press Awards and her stage plays have won national competitions and have been produced in Wisconsin and Virginia. She is currently working on her chapbook *Dancing to Beethoven*.

A.L. ROWSER's short stories appear in *Orca*, *Storm Cellar*, *Bourbon Penn*, *Necessary Fiction*, *The Adroit Journal*, and *The Monarch Review*. She lives with her spouse and three cats in Southern California.

AMY RICHERSON lives in Edgefield, South Carolina.

JESS LUNA, resident of Oklahoma City's Paseo district, stays with their love, Alana, and curious companion, Jimothy. As a ragtag team of proletarians, they face the same struggles we all know. The prominent faces in life change and, sometimes, the ones you always thought would be in your corner . . . just aren't. This "prophecy" is one of generational trauma and taking on the responsibility of breaking the cycle. As with all their writing, chronic illness and disability affect the perspective of the piece. Their free time is spent mostly at home, together. Taking it one day at a time, the dynamic duo spare no effort in creative expression. The apartment, decorated in the nouvous style, and the various musical instruments scattered about signal this well. In small ways, they hope to keep effecting change in their world, and perhaps in today's readers. So, they'll keep writing . . . writing . . . writing . . .

Made in the USA
Middletown, DE
04 June 2022

66484279R00130